Sermons *on the* Great Feasts *of* the Lord

Copyright © 2021 by Patristic Nectar Publications
ALL RIGHTS RESERVED
Printed in the USA

Illustrations by Predrag Ilievski. Drawings by Vladimir and Goce Ilievski.
All interior illustrations and artwork, Copyright © Newrome Press.

Publisher's Cataloging-In-Publication Data

Names: Filaret, Metropolitan of Moscow, 1782-1867, author. | Ilievski, Predrag, illustrator. | Ilievski, Vladimir, 1989- illustrator. | Ilievski, Goce, illustrator. | Kotar, Nicholas, translator.
Title: Sermons on the great feasts of the Lord / Saint Philaret of Moscow ; [illustrations by Predrag Ilievski ; drawings by Vladimir and Goce Ilievski] ; [translated by Deacon Nicholas Kotar].
Other Titles: Sermons. Selections. English
Description: [Riverside, California] : [Patristic Nectar Publications], [2021]
Identifiers: ISBN 9781735011615
Subjects: LCSH: Russkaia͡ pravoslavnai͡a͡ t͡s͡erkov'--Sermons. | Fasts and feasts--Russkai͡a͡ pravoslavnai͡a͡ t͡s͡erkov'. | Sermons, Russian.
Classification: LCC BX513 .F552 2021 | DDC 252.019--dc23

SAINT PHILARET OF MOSCOW

Sermons *on the* Great Feasts *of* the Lord

Contents

Foreword vii
Introduction ix

HOMILIES ON THE HOLY NATIVITY

1. Homily (1811) 1
2. Homily (1812) 7
3. Homily (1821) 14
4. Homily (1823) 21
5. Homily (1824) 26
6. Homily (1826) 32
7. Homily (1834) 38

HOMILIES ON THE HOLY TRANSFIGURATION

8. Homily (1820) 44
9. Homily (1826) 54
10. Homily (1845) 60

HOMILY ON PALM SUNDAY

11. Homily (1825) 66

HOMILIES ON HOLY PASCHA

12. Homily (1811) 74
13. Homily (1822) 79
14. Homily (1824) 84

15. Homily (1825) 92
16. Homily (1826) 101
17. Homily (1827) 105
18. Homily (1842) 112
19. Homily (1844) 118
20. Homily (1845) 124

HOMILIES ON THE HOLY ASCENSION

21. Homily (1824) 130
22. Homily (1825) 138
23. Homily (1854) 145

HOMILIES ON HOLY PENTECOST

24. Homily (1811) 152
25. Homily (1814) 161
26. Homily (1842) 169

Foreword

It is with continued great joy that Patristic Nectar Publications offers this second volume of St. Philaret of Moscow's homilies entitled *Sermons on the Great Feasts of the Lord*. St. Philaret of Moscow was a magnificent preacher of the Gospel. Here in these precious sermons on the Great Feasts of the Lord we are treated to a banquet of inspired proclamation on the great and saving acts of our Lord Jesus Christ. In these pages St. Philaret leads the attentive Christian by the hand to a deep understanding of the work that Jesus Christ our Lord has accomplished for the salvation of mankind. Here, in these pages, we find the measure of God's love for fallen and falling mankind, and the antidote to sin and death. Let your heart drink deeply.

   Father Josiah Trenham
   Patristic Nectar Publications

Introduction

If we examine the history of salvation, we can see that from the beginning the same phenomenon is repeated. Every work begins with the power of God and ends with the seal of His grace. When God completed His creation, He entered into His eternal Sabbath, His eternal rest, thus anointing the creation with the seal of the perfection of the Holy Spirit. Ever since, in the course of the whole sacred history, nothing is achieved nor completed unless a particular kind of prayer precedes, as it is already expressed in the Old Testament in a perfect way: 'Be ye still, and know that I am God' (cf. Ps. 46:10). The spirit of this wondrous and especial stillness is of great importance in performing every work of God. We see then, that the whole nature of our Church is characterised by this spirit.

We have said a few words about the life and greatness of the charismatic Hierarch Philaret in the Introduction of the first volume of this collection. This greatness lies in the fact that this wise Hierarch assimilated and knew the language of God in a perfect way and through his prayer he was able to enter in the heart of the great mystery of godliness that was revealed and 'delivered once unto the saints' (cf. Jude 1:3).

According to his biographer, Saint Philaret would keep vigil for half a night in hesychastic prayer. Thus, he was always prepared to celebrate the Mystery of Divine Eucharist and impart the divine word. Just as the Son and Word of God was born of the stillness of the Father without beginning, so also the word of grace that regenerates the souls of men is born of the stillness of the sanctified hearts that pronounce them.

Stillness begets the word. Yet it also renders palpable the presence of the personal God Whom we honour and worship at every feast. Every Sunday we lay aside every external work in order to abide in the presence of God through prayer and the study of His words. Likewise, at every feast that commemorates the eternal events of the life of the Lord Jesus, we prepare ourselves with the same tension of hesychastic prayer so as to acquire the perfect bond of love with the Person of our Beloved God, Who 'left naught undone until He has lifted us to heaven and bestowed upon us His Kingdom to come'.

Living in the tumult of this world and drowning in a sea of earthly cares, we easily lose the strength and inspiration that we received from God. This is the reason why feasts were instituted throughout the year in order to continue in the same work that we do every Sunday, namely, keeping the precious time of stillness so that in our personal contact with God we may receive His mighty help, that we may know Him more deeply, love Him more tenderly and follow Him more faithfully.

Fruitful participation in the feasts depends on our right vision, our knowledge, love, desire and preparation. When we have Holy Communion in the Divine Liturgy during the feasts of the Lord, our benefit is double because of the great grace wherewith their atmosphere is stirred up.

Through prayerful preparation for the feasts, the time of our worship is overshadowed by the grace of God, which leads us into the presence of the divine Person Whom we honour and glorify. By this grace, we enter eternal events whose contemporaries we become in the Holy Spirit. The feasts are neither a psychological nor an intellectual re-enactment, but a prayerful commemoration and spiritual initiation into the mystery of the Saviour God. We participate in the Holy Spirit, if we offer thanksgiving and make our entreaty, which are two alternating kinds of prayer during the Divine Liturgy.

Moreover, the feasts were given to us so that we may remember the benefits of God. This memory begets gratitude in our heart, and we respond with thanksgiving and entreaty for God to help us on the way of the Cross that leads to salvation. It fights against two of the worst passions, ingratitude and forgetfulness of God, which infest the soul with despondency and end up slaying it altogether.

The feasts are luminous signs of the divine goodness, where eternity overshadows and seals the temporary, so that time may stand and acquire value in eternity, and not be thrust into the darkness of non-existence.

Archimandrite Zacharias
Holy Stavropegic Monastery of St. John the Baptist
Essex, England
2021

1

Homily on the Nativity of the Lord (1811)

Great is the mystery of godliness;
God was manifested in the flesh (1 Tim 3:16).

The new Adam blossoms forth from virginal soil. Woman, the source of the curse, produces the dew of blessing. The true Noah appears who *will comfort us concerning our work and the toil of our hands, because of the ground which the Lord has cursed*. The Melchizedek without genealogy, born without a mother, born without a father, comes to inherit the Kingdom and the eternal Priesthood. Finally, the long night of fear and of mankind's expectation is coming to an end, and the light of morning seeps into the darkness of the Holy Places of the Old Testament, which opens not to the daily East but to the eternal East. The manna of Heaven overflows from the vessel keeping it hidden. The rod of Jesse flowers instead of the withering staff of Aaron.

Genesis 5:29;
Hebrews 7:3

Christ is born!

Come, meek pastors, and kiss the Lamb and the Shepherd—the Lamb that shepherds the shepherds, and the Shepherd that is capable of uniting into a single peaceful flock, wolves with sheep and lions with lambs. Come, you wise men, and bow down before the mysteries of the ancient Child. Learn from the silent Child, and taste of angelic bread from the table of the Unspeakable One, and see how good the Lord is. The hosts of the heavenly powers who proclaimed the Lord *when the morning stars sang together* now multiply Your glorification before the Sun who rises for both you and us.

Job 38:7

Christ is born!

Christ is born in Bethlehem. Does today's joy, with all its "glory to God in the highest," consist in this alone? Glory to God, for He is born for us also for, as the powers would have it, *For unto us a Child is born, unto us a Son is given.* In the midst of the celebration of His birth, the Church suffers birth pangs, awaiting the moment when *Christ is formed in [us].* Let us not despise the joyful sorrow of our Mother. Let us copy at least several motifs from the icon of the birth of Jesus and place them in our hearts.

Isaiah 9:6

Galatians 4:19

Bethlehem was the birthplace of the ancestors of Jesus, however, Joseph and Mary had no more than a poor hut in that town and no permanent place of residence. Providence, by the hand of Caesar, brought them to this place, from which it was foreordained that a Ruler should come who would shepherd *My people Israel.* Foreigners in the land of their ancestors, these travelers in their own homeland, gave birth to the Son of the One *from whom the whole family in Heaven and Earth is named.*

Matthew 2:6

Ephesians 3:15

O Christians! While we live in the world with the carelessness of citizens and enjoy the world with all the power of those who own it as a possession, Christ will never be able to be formed in us. The world constantly tries to stamp the impressions of passing images in our souls; satiated desires give rise to still more desires, which unnoticeably grow into giants that build Babylon. *Blessed is he who takes and dashes the little ones* of this Babylon against the stone of faith and separates himself from the city that abides here, in order to seek the city that comes! If Abraham, by God's command, had not left his country and his people, he would not

Psalm 137:9

have received the glorious covenant, the promise, and the inheritance. If suffering Israel hadn't decided to subject themselves to the difficulties of the dangerous and unknown road through the wilderness, Jehovah would not have come down in power and would not have prepared for Himself a home among them.

If the prescient mother had not sent innocent Jacob away from the wrath of Esau, he would not have come to the frightening place of the "gates of Heaven." Only the homeless wanderers find Bethel and Bethlehem—the house of God and the home of the living Bread. Only willing exiles from the world will be accepted as citizens of Heaven. Whoever desires to be in the house of the Son of God, he must have his inheritance in God alone and, in spite of all his attachments to the land of his fathers (even if it is entirely natural and just), he must prefer it only as the threshold of Heaven.

Jesus, not having borrowed anything from the world in His birth, apparently did not want to show the world anything extraordinary. The Carpenter received His father's name; she who bore Him in her womb, by her own admission, brought to this service no other dignity than a sense of her own unworthiness: *He has regarded the lowly state of His maidservant.* He hid His immeasurable eternity behind the day of His birth. The throne of the King of kings became a manger. The riches of the King became swaddling clothes. The first servants of the Kingdom were the shepherds of the flocks. God's power and wisdom were hidden in the weakness of a Child. But who can measure the distance from the height of the divine essence to the depths of His humility? The finite mind cannot comprehend Him, either in the height above all heavens, or in His descent to the abyss of our fallen nature. What must the heart feel, seeing such humility, and desiring to be like the image of Jesus?

Luke 1:48

The power of the mind, the greatness of the spirit, the fame of deeds, the advantages of a high calling—I do not find these to be desirable, and I do not envy those who are proud of them.

There is no higher wisdom than to reject wisdom for the sake of Jesus. There is no greater glory than to share dishonor with Jesus. There is no higher state than the poverty of Jesus. There is no more beautiful adornment of the soul, in which Christ must abide, than to see yourself lacking all adornment, just like His manger. The flow of grace, like a driving river, pours out into valleys; the cedars on the mountains are subject to thunder and lightning. God creates out of nothing: as long as we desire to become anyone of significance, He will not even begin His work in us. Humility and rejection of self is the foundation of His temple within us. The deeper you lay the foundation, the higher and more secure the edifice.

One of the essential aspects of the birth of Jesus was the purity of His Mother, which was transgressed neither by gaze nor even by thought. She had to have a betrothed, but only so that he could be her protector and a witness to her virginity, and so that her holy virginity would not seem to be a condemnation of marriage. All the while she remained, as the Church has maintained with a single voice, a virgin both before birth-giving, in birth-giving, and after birth-giving. Look at her example, O soul that strives to unite with God, and see what you must do in the mirror of her perfection. The Lord is a jealous God. While with a voice of fatherly goodwill He says to man, *My son, give me your heart*, His righteous zeal commands, both in a spiritual and a moral sense, *Do not commit adultery*. He who has given us a heart is not content either with a large or a small portion of it—it must belong completely to the Lord of all.

Proverbs 23:26
Exodus 20:14

He does not consider worthy of Himself any love that is not founded on love for Him, any pleasure in which we seek to passionately grab something for ourselves, nor any thought inclined toward created things, for any distraction is a movement away from Him. Only strict vigilance over the self can lead to a blessed union with Him and preserve us in that union: *Keep your heart with all diligence, for out of it spring the issues of life*. The heavenly

Proverbs 4:23

Bridegroom is betrothed only with the wise and pure virgins who do not sleep at the door of His bridal chamber. Only the virginal soul, which turns only to God, can conceive a spiritual life and give birth to the blessedness of pure contemplation. *Blessed are the pure in heart, for they shall see God.* And where? In their own hearts! The pure heart, like clean water, will accept into itself the living images of the sun and the sky. *Matthew 5:8*

Let us not hold our glances any longer on those aspects of the icon of the birth of Jesus that might inspire fear in the souls of those who wish to emulate the life of Jesus. But let us look one final time at how His divine glory shone forth through His humiliation, which is an image of how we receive grace through our spiritual birth.

During the birth of Christ, the Angels sang about the glory of God and peace on Earth. They also declared the glory of grace and peace between man and God during our spiritual rebirth. *There will be more joy in Heaven over one sinner who repents than over ninety-nine just persons who need no repentance.* The shepherds and the magi come with reverence to Christ, in spite of the poverty and lack of notoriety that seemed to separate Him from the rest of the world. In the same way, the one who unites with Christ unites also, in Him, with all those who are faithful to Him with the same unbreakable bond. The same Spirit that forms them into a single community––or better yet, a single body––sometimes in an unintended fashion, but always at the proper time, brings them together to teach and learn, to comfort and be comforted, and to confess the mercy and glory of God *Luke 15:7*

Gifts are brought to Christ, as to a king. Frankincense, as to God, and myrrh, as to the One to die for mortals. But did He not also promise to us that to those who seek the Kingdom of God, *all these things will be added to you?* Does He not want to make us *kings and priests to His God and Father?* Does He not unite our spiritual birth with His life-giving death, after which our life will be *hidden with Christ in God?* *Matthew 6:33* *Revelation 1:6* *Colossians 3:3*

O God, who gave us Your Son! What gifts do you not give us, together with Him? Give us this gift alone: for the Spirit of Christ to be born in us, and for us to live through His life. Then let Herod and all of Jerusalem rise up against us, as they once did against Him. Let the prince of this world bluster, and let this world raise arms against us. You will cover us in the mystery of Your dwelling place; on the waters of rest will You nurture us, and through the Angel of Your covenant will you lead us to Your holy mountain. Amen.

A Homily on the Nativity of Christ (1812)

And this shall be a sign to you; you shall find the Babe wrapped in swaddling clothes, lying in a manger (Luke 2:12).

For three days, the Church has glorified and proclaimed the *born Savior* in altars and in homes. The shepherds in Bethlehem, having heard the heavenly news for hardly three seconds, immediately hastened to find Him: *the shepherds said one to another, 'Let us now go even unto Bethlehem, and see this thing which is come to pass, which the Lord hath made known unto us.'* We have already heard the words of glorification many times, and have been called ourselves to glorify the newborn Christ: "Christ is born, glorify Him." We are almost physically pushed to welcome Christ: "Christ comes from Heaven; come to welcome Him!" Have we finally made it Bethlehem? Have we seen the promised Savior?

Luke 2:11

Luke 2:15

Will those who neither have the simple-hearted faith of the shepherds of Bethlehem, nor the wisdom of the magi from the East, tell us how to get to Bethlehem? Can we allow ourselves to remain further from our newborn Savior than pagan wise men, or in greater ignorance than the simple-minded shepherds? The Church does not lie when she cries out, "Christ comes from Heaven; come to welcome Him!"

Of course, Christ descends to us this very moment and is so close to us that we can draw near to the place of His divine manifestation. "Let us now go even unto Bethlehem." "Bethlehem" means "house of bread" – what other bread could it be but the "living bread which came down from Heaven?" (John 6:51). Every Christian soul must come to *this* Bethlehem. Every Christian soul should strive to become a house for this Bread, so that eventually we may all enter into the *new Jerusalem*, the *tabernacle of God*.

Apocalypse 21:2-3

Galatians 1:16

God wants to *reveal his Son* in all of us through our rebirth in His grace. And so, in order to find the path to the newborn Savior, and to prevent ourselves from being corrupted by the old Jerusalem (which, on the day of salvation, revolted with Herod to its own destruction), let us hurry to ask: what visible sign can assure us of our own closeness to Christ, of the truth of our spiritual rebirth?

In the Gospel, we find two paths to the newborn Christ: the path of the magi and the path of the shepherds. The path of the magi is one of light and pursuit, guided by the clear sign of the star that they saw in the East and that led them to Jerusalem and Bethlehem. The path of the shepherds is one of hidden mystery, a path of faith. It does not include any obvious sign that appears during the night's vigil, nor any revelation of the glory of the Lord. Such a path is taken without guidance or without any miraculous sign, nothing but these words: *And this shall be a sign unto you; you shall find the Babe wrapped in swaddling clothes, lying in a manger.*

Luke 2:12

Perhaps, then, it seems that the path of the wise men is safer, more convenient, even shorter? Quite the contrary! It was longer, more difficult, and more dangerous than the secret path of the shepherds. After all, the magi arrived first in Jerusalem, not Bethlehem. Here the announcement of the sign they saw in the heavens produced nothing but general upheaval. The magi, distressed, didn't even know where their path should lead them next. The guidance of the heavenly sign became unclear to them, and the heavenly Child before whom they desired to fall down in awe nearly fell into the hands of the unrighteous.

The shepherds passed over fields of darkness and reached Bethlehem, coming upon the glory of the Lord that once illuminated them from the heavens and now invisibly entered into them: *And the shepherds returned, glorifying and praising God.* Luke 2:20

Let us glorify the glorious path of the wise men, but let us not scorn the path of the shepherds either. If the bright path of guidance attracts our gazes, let us not forget that we must not merely be observers, but careful travelers. While our eyes are lost looking at the majestic sight before us, it's easy to forget about the rocks, snares, and chasms beneath our feet, or even to stop in our tracks when we should be moving forward. Thus, we can't always assume that a bright illumination of our mind is an undisputable sign of our closeness to Christ. Such a state is not always a faithful indicator of the true path to rebirth. There are some spirits who receive and transmit light but do not feel it themselves. They can even create fire in others while they remain dead and cold themselves. Even the greatest human wisdom is like such spirits, since it travels down a still unmarked path. And so, human wisdom is an unreliable guide. If at times that path is brightly lit, at others it is completely dark.

However, how can we expect anything else? We aren't yet destined for true and living vision. For us, a blessed life consists in faith: *For we walk by faith, not by sight,* and *blessed are they that have not seen, and yet have believed.* Let us follow the footsteps of the 2 Corinthians 5:7
John 20:29

shepherds of Bethlehem who walk the mysterious path of faith. The more hidden and invisible it is, the more we should find our way forward by touch, seeking tactile signs.

After all, only those who have already walked, seen, and measured these dark paths can leave clear and obvious signs for followers. And who can see, reveal, and signal the path of pure rebirth, *not of blood, nor of the will of the flesh,* other than the One who alone was born sinless? The One who was overshadowed by the Holy Spirit and the power of the Most High? Only He who gives *power to become the sons of God* to His followers can be the trailblazer.

John 1:13

Luke 1:35

John 1:12

For this reason, He was born on Earth, to give us heavenly rebirth. He was visibly born to reveal the invisible birth to us mortals. And since He was born in purity and holiness, He had no need to embark upon the path of rebirth. And so, He made His fleshly birth a translucent *veil* through which we can look through at the new and living path of our spiritual rebirth. You no longer need to beg God with David's words: *Cause me to know the way wherein I should walk.* The unseen path is declared visibly by the incarnate Word of God: *I am the way.*

Hebrews 10:20

Psalm 143:8

John 14:6

O Wisdom of the heights! Do not even think of following any paths of ascent to God within your hearts other than the path by which the Son of God descended to man. *Let this mind be in you, which was also in Christ Jesus: who, being in the form of God, thought it not robbery to be equal with God: but made himself of no reputation, and took upon himself the form of a servant, and was made in the likeness of men.* Do not walk quickly past this sign that reveals itself in unadorned humility in Bethlehem of Judea. For your own personal Bethlehem is sealed within His humility. The inner sign of our awakening to salvation is made manifest in the outer sign of the newborn Savior.

Philippians 2:5-7

First of all, *this shall be a sign unto you; you shall find the Babe.* When man embraced the pride of Satan, he became a giant, for whom the *strait gate* and *narrow way, which leads to life* became

Luke 2:12

Matthew 7:14

impossible. To make the straight and narrow path passable for men again, the Son of God humbled His immense greatness to the size of a mere infant. And so, he shows us a way to pass through the gate to the way of life and to approach the gates of the Kingdom.

The question that His disciples at one time asked Him: *Who is greatest in the Kingdom of Heaven?* was already taught by Him by the complete silence of His infancy: *Except you be converted, and become as little children....* Thus, whoever wants to attain the path of Jesus must emulate His humility. The Babe rests in the arms of His mother, thinks through her mind, is controlled by her will, is fed by her food, and lives by her life. If you assume the childlike simplicity to find comfort in the arms of Providence, if your mind forgets itself in reverent humility before the providence of God, if you do the will of God as though it were your own, if ycu *desire the sincere milk of the word* not only as something pleasant but as the food of renewal and revitalization of the spirit—then you will bless God, who instilled the living sign of Christ's birth within you. *Matthew 18:1,3* *1 Peter 2:2*

Secondly, *You shall find the Babe wrapped.* The sign of the wrapping of the infant in swaddling clothes is explained to us by Tertullian.[1] He says that by being wrapped in swaddling clothes, Jesus began His entombment. The swaddling clothes of the babe and the shroud of the dead are woven by the same artisan; the cradle and tomb share the same source. Had sin not produced the tomb and the shroud, then there would not have been any wrappings or cradle. The difficulties of birth are actually the beginning of death, and so the cradle is the forerunner of the tomb, and the swaddling clothes are the first strand of the funeral shroud. *Luke 2:12*

Why does the Son of God, who wills to be wrapped in swaddling clothes, provide through them a symbol of a life of con-

---

1 Tertullian, *Contra Marcion*, book IV

stant mortification? No matter who you are, if you wish to follow Jesus, you must also cross the valley of the shadow of death on your way to rebirth in eternal life. Every temptation must be *cut off*, every movement of self-will must be ceased, every worldly lust put to death: *Mortify therefore your members which are upon the Earth.*

> Matthew 18:8
>
> Colossians 3:5

Like the One wrapped in clothes, you must guard your inner freedom, you must open your proverbial eyes only to look calmly at the bonds of your old man, and by doing so, you must come to mortify your vision itself. You must guard your lips so that they only breathe the exclamations of prayer. This is how the faithful followers of the Lord *bore about in the body the dying of the Lord Jesus and died daily.* However, in this very death, they partook of new life: *As dying, and, behold, we live.* A life of self-mortification is an obvious sign that you follow the path of Christ, for the tomb of the old man is the cradle of the new.

> 2 Corinthians 4:10;
> 1 Corinthians 15:31;
> 2 Corinthians 6:9

Finally, *And this shall be a sign unto you; you shall find the Babe wrapped in swaddling clothes, lying in a manger.* If the infancy and swaddling-clothes of the God-man are a sign of His deep humility and death, then His manger is a depiction of his inconceivable self-emptying. He already diminished Himself before the Angels through his humanity. By assuming infancy and the swaddling clothes, He assumed that which is most demeaning in mankind.

> Luke 2:12

He descended even further than that, and then the Word that was inseparably *with God* was found with the irrational beasts. How is it possible for everything exalted in men, everything glorious in the world, to do anything but shrink, crumble, and disappear into its natural worthlessness before this sign of divine kenosis?

> John 1:1

Blessed is he who venerates the manger of the God-man in the same way he venerates the throne of His Majesty. Let him lose the whole world, let him lose himself in the boundless depth of his own nothingness, for this boundless depth is the place where he can commune with the eternal Divinity. In the words of the Psalmist, let his *soul faint for [his] salvation*. *Psalm 119:81*

Do you see how the sign of the newborn Savior in Bethlehem is not only given to the shepherds from Bethlehem but to every one of us, to lead us on our spiritual path to Christ the Savior? I will ask once more: have we come to Bethlehem? What does our soul search for? Have we sought Him with the same relentlessness, tirelessness, and faithfulness as the humble shepherds that *came with haste, and found* Him? *Luke 2:16*

O, the infancy of Jesus! How difficult it seems to us to empty ourselves to Your humble state! We do not love diminishing ourselves with You. Rather, we prefer self-aggrandizement—to grow in self-will, sinful desires, and false glory. O, the life woven in burial! How often do we thoughtlessly trample and boldly tear apart your swaddling clothes! We desire to live instead of dying, instead of dying to be-born into new life.

O the Wisdom and Word of God, teaching us even now from the manger! How little do we listen to the great sermon of Your silence! It is as though we consider the signs of the Son of God to be too insignificant and humiliating. It is as though we would prefer instead to see *the sign of the Son of man in Heaven*. Oh yes, *Matthew 24:30* that sign will appear, but then it will be neither a time of celebration nor learning: *then shall all the tribes of the Earth mourn.* *Matthew 24:30*

Let us make haste, O Christians, to walk the shaded path of faith, so that the light of the Day of Judgment does not blind us. Let us greet Christ, who descended from Heaven for us, with love. Then, He will greet us with mercy as we ascend to the heavens. If anyone has already come to him with the shepherds, let him return from the glory of the King back to the simplicity of faith, glorifying the one God. If anyone has come to Bethlehem from Jerusalem with the magi, let him *not return to Herod* to boast of *Matthew 2:12* what he found. Let not the mystery of the King of glory be made a weapon for the rulers of the darkness of this world that *seek the young Child to destroy him.* Amen *Matthew 2:13*

3

Homily on the Nativity, in remembrance of the salvation of the Church and the Russian Empire from the invasion of the French (1821)

*And suddenly there was with the Angel
a multitude of the heavenly host praising God and saying,
Glory to God in the highest (Luke 2:13)!*

Today the Angels prophesy to us, O Christians, and they themselves demonstrate for us what we must do, according to their prophecy. What can be better than this instruction, and is there any other instruction necessary after it? An Angel appears and preaches to mankind: *Behold, I bring you good tidings of great joy which will be to all people. For there is born to you this day in the city of David a Savior, who is Christ the Lord.* Mankind should have answered this joyful preaching with this exclamation, "Amen!", and glorified God for this good news. But it is the Angels that appear as listeners to the angelic prophecy. As soon as the first Angel uttered the good

Luke 2:10-11

news of Christ's birth, they answered in a loud choir: "Glory to God in the highest!" They cried out so loudly that not only the heavenly realm, their home, rang out with their doxology, but the Earth below did also.

And for what reason? Without a doubt, it was so that the world below would follow the world above, so that human doxology would follow angelic singing. And so, let us be obedient to the angelic instruction: *Oh come, let us sing to the Lord! Let us shout joyfully to the God of our salvation!* Glory to God in the Highest! But you have already come to rejoice in the birth of the Savior. The glorification that the Church assumed from the Angels is not only sounded in the churches of God but in your very homes. The angelic announcement, in spite of the fact that it was uttered so many centuries ago, still reveals its power. It seems as though the event occurs at this very moment.

Psalm 94:1

In fact, it would be wise for earthly servants of the world to be silent and calm when the preachers of Heaven act. But their preaching is short and filled with meaning, and their glorification is sudden. They unwittingly inspire us to wonder, and through wonder to examination and contemplation. Moreover, we are led to the thought that when the heavenly powers preached and celebrated the birth of our Savior, only a few shepherds listened, while the entirety of the lower world was plunged into sleep and did not hear their words or their doxology. Is it possible, some may ask, that even we can sleep through the great doxology of the Church in the middle of the brightness of the Lord's Day?

Without rebuking anyone, I will only remind you that David, who, without a doubt, was far more vigilant than we in doxology, found it necessary sometimes to arouse himself to prayer: *Awake, my glory!* And so we must also, as we contemplate the glory of God and the birth of our Savior, awake our glory, or, better yet, arouse our zeal for glorifying God.

Psalm 56:9

Glory to God in the Highest!

Never before the birth of Jesus Christ did the Earth hear such an angelic doxology. And why never before? Did the Lord not have glory in the highest before then?

Of course He did! God had the greatest glory from the beginning of the ages. According to one witness of His glory, He is *The God of glory*, that is, glory is connected with His very Name, with His very essence, so that He would not be God if He did not have glory.

Acts 7:2

Glory is a revelation, a manifestation, a reflection, an externalization of inner perfection. God, from eternity, is revealed to Himself in the eternal birth of the Son of God, and in the eternal procession of the Holy Spirit, both of whom are one in essence with the Father. In this way, His unity in the Holy Trinity shines forth essentially in an undimmed and unchanging glory. God the Father is the *Father of glory*, the Son of God is the *brightness of His glory*, and Himself has *the glory which [He] had with [the Father]...before the world was*. Equally, the Spirit of God is the *Spirit of glory*. The blessed God who is above all glory abides in His own internal glory, so that He does not require any other witnesses and does not need any participants in His glory. However, since, by His endless goodness and love, He desires to communicate His blessedness, to have gracious participants in His glory, He moved outward with His endless perfections, and they are manifested in His creation. His glory appears to the heavenly powers, is reflected in mankind, and is dressed in the beauty of the visible world. He gives it, and it is accepted by its participants, and then it returns to Him, and this circle of the glory of God comprises the blessed life and the prosperity of creation.

Ephesians 1:17
Hebrews 1:3
John 17:5
1 Peter 4:14

This is how the Cherubim stand before the throne of the Lord, in the fullness of His glory, and they exclaim to one another in doxology of the Holy Trinity, *Holy, Holy, Holy, Lord of Sabaoth*. They close their faces because the essential glory of God is *unapproachable light* even for the higher creations. They are *full of eyes around and within* because the desire to commune with the glory of God through contemplation makes their entire essence eye-like. They

Isaiah 6:3

1 Timothy 4:16
Revelation 4:8

do not rest day or night, not because they have been forbidden to have any rest, but because the blessedness that fills their contemplation of, and participation in, the glory of God, as though from an overfilled vessel, constantly flows in a joyful babbling of doxology. *Revelation 4:8*

In this way, *the honor that comes from the only God* returns to God. Thus man, who in his original creation was *the image and glory of God*, knew not nakedness, though he was without clothing, because he was dressed in the same glory. Thus, the visible heavens *declare the glory of God...day unto day utters speech, and night unto night reveals knowledge.* *John 5:44* *1 Corinthians 11:7* *Psalm 18:2-3*

But if in this way the glory of God abides in God from the ages, and if it is announced constantly and from the ages both in the creation itself (not only in the invisible but in the visible creation as well), then why was it announced in a new and unexpected way at the birth of Jesus Christ, announced from Heaven to Earth, as though it were something unknown and unheard-of? O Christian! Now it is your turn to be the "eye," especially an "inner eye," and so stand upright and contemplate: here is both the glory and the mystery, the glory hidden in the mystery, and the mystery revealed in glory.

Mankind stopped the eternally living doxology of God within himself, deciding not to offer it to God, but to ascribe it to himself instead, in the hope that the promise of the seducer— *You will be as gods*—would come true. Therefore, in the spiritual man, something happened similar to what happens in the physical man when blood ceases to circulate. Man died, spiritually speaking, to the glory of God, or at the very least he became so hardened that only a weak remnant of the spiritual life was left inside him, and it was darkened, naked, sickly, and perishable. *Genesis 3:5*

In this visible world, the glory of God spread primarily through mankind, reflected as it was in him, the image of God. Therefore, having hidden itself from man, it no longer shines as brightly through the natural world as it once did. The Psalmist, having purified his senses, afterward heard the voice of the heavens that declare the glory of God and their sound going out over all the Earth. However, that sound is neither as exalted or majestic as it was in the beginning, for then only the majestic and sweet sounds of life and harmony were heard, but now, added to these, we still hear the admixture of the sounds of suffering and the noise of destruction. Mankind, darkened by sin, accomplished this sad dimming of the glory of God on Earth by submerging all their desires and thoughts into the created world, *and [they] changed the glory of the incorruptible God into an image made like corruptible man—and birds and four-footed animals and creeping things.* [Romans 1:23]

The God of glory, knowing that without His glory there is no blessedness for His creatures, used (we will use merely human language) many different and unusual means to reveal it in people. However, for a long time, these efforts seemed to be in vain, while in actual fact they were only more or less distant and temporary preparations for the actual, universal, and only possible revelation of His glory among those who were lacking it, because all sinned. [Romans 3:23] In the very first moments of man's separation from the glory of God, God sought man, that He could return His glory to him: *Adam, where are you?* [Genesis 3:9] But the sinner could not bear its presence any longer; he fled and hid from it.

Afterward, in order to make it possible for people to accept it, God sometimes clothed His glory in the revelations of Angels, but even this brought human nature to terror, and could not serve as a mediation for communion with God's glory: *Alas, O Lord God! For I have seen the Angel of the Lord face to face.* [Judges 6:22] *And Manoah said to his wife, 'We shall surely die, because we have seen God!* [Judges 13:22] The nation of Israel, no matter how assiduously prepared, through God's direct instruction mediated by Moses, for the revelation of God's glory on Sinai, couldn't bear it, even standing at a distance: *They said to Moses, 'You speak with us, and we will hear; but let not God speak with us, lest we die'.* [Exodus 20:19]

And what shall we say of those manifestations of God's glory, when the degree of man's iniquity, and the groaning going up to

God as a result, was so great that He could not, without betraying His holiness, answer with a voice of love and compassion, but only with a voice of the threatening and stern fates of His justice, as happened, for example, in the condemnation of Cain, during the Flood, and in the destruction of Sodom? *The God of glory thunders*, the earth quakes; man disappears. How could anyone rejoice? Who was left to glorify? Psalm 28:3

Finally, what does the God who is limitless in His mercy and salvation do, to restore man into the hope of glory? Since man did not dare approach God to commune of His glory, God came close to man and communed of his humiliation. Lest the sinner flee the presence of God again, the Son of God appeared to him *in the likeness of sinful flesh*. Lest His creation, weak as it was, simply disappear at the revelation of the glory of the all-powerful Creator, He is no longer *clothed with honor and majesty*, but in the weakness and inability of childhood and in poverty-stricken swaddling clothes. As a talented doctor who sees that the sick person is afraid of strong medicine, He hides his medicine in a different form. And thus, the medicine is taken and the sick person is saved. This is why the heavenly Physician of souls and bodies, seeing that mankind, infected with the death-bearing sickness of sin, was afraid of the divine (and this in spite of the fact that nothing other than the divine could heal him), hid His divinity in the form of man.

Romans 8:3

Psalm 104:1

And thus, the human race, before we even knew it, tasted the divine, the all-healing medicine of grace. As soon as the divine entered the human, *His divine power [gave] to us all things that pertain to life and godliness, through the knowledge of Him who called us by glory and virtue*. Therefore, our weakness is made strong in the power of God. Our falsehood is removed by the righteousness of God. Our darkness is enlightened by the light of God. Our death will be trampled down by the life of God. In the very hiding of the glory of God, we find the hope of glory; when this glory will be revealed, it will no longer blind or terrify or break us. On the

2 Peter 1:3

contrary, having shone forth within us, it will then give light to the whole world which we ourselves have made dark. *Do you now know yourselves, that Jesus Christ is in you?* This is the encouragement of the Apostle.

2 Corinthians 13:5

This is the glorious mystery and mysterious power of this day! Heavenly servants of the light saw the dawning of this glory before we ever did, and immediately, having turned to Him, they declared, *Glory to God in the highest!* Now it is no longer the morning, but the full day of this glory. Let our own doxology rise up. Let it go up also to the inhabitants of Heaven. Let our own words rise up in the joyful ecstasy of the heart to the very throne of the Almighty: Glory to God in the highest!"

Brethren! Consider that the Angels glorified God so triumphantly not for their salvation, but for our own! With equal zeal should we glorify God for our own selves! Who will give me a spark of heavenly fire, of angelic love for God, so that I may light your own hearts to the angelic, never-silent, never-ending doxology of God? For I know that the world is preparing to dim within you even an inkling of angelic doxology through the noise of parties, pointless conversations, songs that dissipate the purity of spirit, and *with carousing, drunkenness, and cares of this life.*

Luke 21:34

Be careful that you do not insult God, your Savior, whom you glorified with your words in church, and by your deeds at home. *For those who honor Me I will honor, and those who despise Me shall be lightly esteemed.* And have we not already experienced this dishonor heavily, so that the Lord not only abandoned our homes to plunder and fire, but even left behind His churches? For what other reason, except that we humiliated Him in our homes by lives unworthy of His glory, and humiliated Him in our churches by laziness in performing works of piety? But behold! He again had mercy and glorified us all. Let us then glorify Him, lest we once again inspire His anger against us, as we often do because of the extraordinarily fickle nature of our humanity. *To God give the glory! Glorify God in your body and in your spirit, which are God's.*

1 Kingdoms 2:30

Psalm 67:35;
1 Corinthians 6:20

4

Homily on the Nativity of Christ (1823)

Now when they had seen Him,
they made widely known the saying which was told them
concerning this Child. And all those who heard it marveled
at those things which were told them
by the shepherds (Luke 2:17-18).

Is there anyone left who is still not amazed by these words concerning Jesus Christ's birth, even though, after so many centuries, not only the simple shepherds of irrational sheep, but also the wise shepherds of the rational flocks have spoken of it nearly on a daily basis? For what do the shepherds of Bethlehem say about Him? They retell the heavenly word, the message of Angels, *for there is born to you this day in the city of David a Savior, who is Christ the Lord.* And if this message inspires you with the desire to find Him and the question of how to come to know Him, the Angels give a further instruction: *This will be a sign to you: You will find a Babe wrapped in swaddling clothes, lying in a manger.*

Luke 2:11

Luke 2:12

O, what a sign this is! Christ is the actual, perfect Anointed One of God, but His sign is not a crown and kingly clothing of glory and honor, but swaddling clothes! He is the Lord; yet, instead of a throne, He lies in a manger! He is the Savior of mankind, but mankind does not give Him the smallest corner to protect His feeble human life; instead, they send Him out to the irrational beasts.

Would you like to hear some of the other things spoken of by the shepherds, who lead their flocks not with staffs, but with teaching and reason? The newly born One is He who Is for all the ages. The Child is the Father of the age to come. He is the Son of Man, but also the Son of a virgin, now and forever a true Son of a virgin, but now, and forever, and to the ages of ages also truly the Son of God. For a short time, He was numbered among the created ones, but He is the One who in the beginning created everything in Heaven and on Earth. Here He lies silent among the irrational beasts, but He is the Word that speaks always and that bears all through the word of His power, the living Word of God, the man Christ Jesus, but at the same time He Who Is above all, God blessed for all ages!

But we could increase our words *ad infinitum* and still not be able to plumb the depths of the Word of God. Even after all words are spoken concerning Him, even unto the end of time, He will still remain un-spoken. Even though all creatures exclaim His glory, from the highest to the lowest places, the Word still remains a mystery. Blessed is the mind, which, having purified the senses and having silenced the passions, can rise up higher than the word to hear the Word, for then He will utter Himself into the silence of that contemplation! No longer daring to speak so crudely with the wise concerning the nature of the Child Who Is, I will once more mention, in the simplest possible way, that this Child appeared for us people.

The Angel spoke the *tidings of great joy*, and the shepherds retold it, *for there is born to you this day... a Savior... [who] will save His people from their sins*. What joyful, what wondrous tidings! What can be more calamitous than sin, the source of all other calam-

Luke 2:10-11; Matthew 1:21

ities? It separates man from God; it establishes enmity between man and man, and between man and nature; it divided us from our own selves.

Sin deprives the soul of peace, the mind of illumination, the body of incorruption, the land of blessing, and all creation of all goodness. It begins by inserting Hell into man, and it ends by imprisoning man in Hell. And so, truly great are these tidings of joy, for finally the One Who will save mankind from their sins has appeared! And what does He do to save us sinners? He is born! From His deathless, divine life, He is born into human life, a mortal life. He sets aside His glory, He leaves behind His blessedness, He hides His holiness and He assumes all the consequences of sin, except for sin itself. *For He made Him who knew no sin to be sin for us, that we might become the righteousness of God in Him.* 2 Corinthians 5:21

Since we did not want to remain blessed children of God in Paradise, He becomes a poor child on Earth. Since we used all our powers and abilities for evil, He now appears without any power or ability. Because our feet ran to deeds of evil, and our hands created the works of unrighteousness, the feet of the One who walks the clouds and the hands of the Pantocrator are tied with swaddling clothes. Our lips speak vanity constantly and our tongues weave lies, so that with our tongue *we bless our God and Father, and with it we curse men, who have been made in the similitude of God.* Because of our irrational cursing and our frivolity of speech, the Word that blesses all remains silent. James 3:9

Man, being in honor, understood it not; he shall be compared unto the brute beasts, and is become like unto them through his bestial passions and animalistic desires. And so, He *who, being in the form of God,* not only *made Himself of no reputation, taking the form of a bondservant, and coming in the likeness of men,* but He even accepted a home and place of rest among those who have no speech at all. Psalm 48:21 Philippians 2:6-7

And what else? *Thus it is fitting for [Him] to fulfill all righteousness,* to fulfill the entire law of God. He does not even transgress a sin- Matthew 3:15

gle human law, and yet still *He was numbered with the transgressors*, so that He might *redeem us from the curse of the Law*, a law which had condemned our actions to Hell and Perdition. The One who was blessed before the ages became *a curse for us*, to raise us up from death. Our own Savior descended to death for us; He was born on Earth not to live, for it was not for life that His earthly birth was necessary. No, He came to die, to plunge heavenly birth into Hell itself, to give birth to life-from-death, to lead the sons of Heaven from Hell, to save the saved from perdition.

Isaiah 53:12
Galatians 3:13

This is how He saves His people from their sin. O Christians! How do you hear and understand these words concerning Christ the Child? Will you not accept these words as did all those people who listened to the shepherds' reports concerning this Child? *And all those who heard it marveled at those things which were told them by the shepherds.* Truly, it would be too frightening and unworthy of us to listen with indifference to the clarion call of the teachings of the Apostles and teachers of the Church, unlike those who didn't listen to the mystical words of the Prophets. Truly, it would be terrible if we paid less attention to the reality of our salvation than those who merely listened to the possibility of its coming. *O Lord, I have heard Your speech and was afraid; You went forth for the salvation of Your people, for salvation with Your Anointed.*

Luke 2:18
Habakkuk 3:2, 13

I will give thanks unto You, for You have fearfully worked wonders; marvelous are Your works, and that my soul knows right well. The Church sings, "How can we fail to be amazed at your giving birth to the God-man, O All-holy Virgin?" However, if you still cannot understand what the best way is to enter into the great event of the Incarnation, do not be afraid to ask how. All those who heard the shepherds of Bethlehem speak of the swaddled child lying in the manger were amazed. But the shepherds left; the wondrous child was hidden; the peoples' wonder ceased; and those who heard of the miracle of the Savior-Child before all others, but who did not understand the mystery and did not follow Him,

Psalm 138:14

soon felt the terrible hand of the persecutor in the destruction of their own children.

Listen to all that you hear me say today, and *take heed how you hear*. I know that your own spiritual pastors do not abandon you; on the contrary, they follow you everywhere with the glory of the Child of Bethlehem. However, the world is constantly making noise to drown your pastors out, and to distract you from the reverent wonder at the miracle of Christ the Child to an unfocused state, to various sensual pleasures and frivolous pursuits, and to deeds that are repugnant to Christ. Be careful, lest Christ, whom you have come to know not only by hearing of His teachings, but by the communion of His mysteries, hide from us again and retreat into His unreachable mystery. Beware, lest His Word, sown in your hearts, be stolen by the enemy, who has his own subtle weapons. Though they are not as cruel as Herod's, they are still effective at destroying the fruits of spiritual birth within you.

Luke 8:18

We must try to be not merely attentive listeners of the word of Christ, but also doers of the works of salvation. Emulate the shepherds who, having heard the voice of the Angel, were not content with mere wonder, but *came with haste and found Mary and Joseph, and the Babe lying in a manger*. Emulate Mary herself, who *kept all these things and pondered them in her heart*. Place the word of the child Jesus in your hearts; and just as a pregnant woman walks carefully and acts in a way not to endanger the child in her womb, so also you must walk and act in the world with care about what you touch and come into contact with, so that nothing can cast out from your hearts the sweet memory and the love given to you by the child Jesus. Do not lose the spirit of salvation that has come to be born in your spirit, which He will nurture in all of you by His grace, entering through faith into your hearts, and abiding there forever. Amen.

Luke 2:16

Luke 2:19

5

Homily on the Nativity (1824)

So all this was done that it might be fulfilled which was spoken by the Lord through the Prophet, saying, 'Behold, the virgin shall be with child, and bear a Son, and they shall call His name Emmanuel,' which is translated, 'God with us' (Matthew 1:22-23).

The holy Evangelist Matthew noted many times that the events and circumstances that signaled the earthly birth and incarnation of our God and Savior Jesus Christ were not simply random occurrences and events, but the exact fulfillment of prophetic words. This is an important point not only for the Jews, who wished only to see events—even those that could be interpreted simply—through the prism of the Prophets, but also for anyone who desires to find the traces of providence in the complex randomness that characterizes human life, or to see the works of God in the events of the world at large. Is it not obviously the work of God when something that has been predicted centuries before occurs with exactness? Especially when the fulfillment of the prophecy is something that by normal conception and understanding appears to be impossible?

Isaiah seems to be pointing at someone standing directly in front of him when he describes the Virgin Mary: "Behold the virgin," he said, even before her parents had so much as appeared on Earth. "Behold, the virgin shall conceive and bear a son." What are you saying, O Prophet? Can a virgin conceive? Can a birth-giver be a virgin? If this is possible, how can it be possible in the nation to whom you gave this prophecy: *The Lord Himself will give you a sign*? If you truly do see this daughter of David that you indicate, if you truly do see her in a country far from the land of David, in despised "Nazareth," an orphan in poverty, with no kingly sign of her breeding, a girl taught to work with her hands... tell me, how can the Lord give a sign that this girl would be the virgin of the house of David, who gives birth in the house and land of David, or, as another Prophet predicted, in *Bethlehem*?   *Isaiah 7:14*

   Micah 5:2

Look how exactly the Lord Himself answers for the veracity of his Prophet's word. *The Holy Spirit ... came upon [her]* and *the power of the Highest* overshadowed her, and she conceived in her womb, while remaining a virgin, and became a mother of a Son, all the while remaining a virgin. So that those who did not know the mystery of this conception might not harm her, she was betrothed to a husband before this conception. And so that every properly-reasoning person would know that this was the sign of the Lord that a virgin conceived without a husband, this conception occurred after the betrothal, *before they came together*, before Joseph took his wife into his house. An Angel was sent to Joseph, lest he remain in confusion, and the mystery was revealed, and the sign was made manifest.   *Luke 1:35*

   Matthew 1:18, 24

As for the others who could not see or hear the Angels, Joseph himself, no less trustworthy than an Angel, served as a true witness of the sign and a messenger of the mystery, for he was everywhere known as a righteous man who would not delude people, much less lie before God and the Holy Spirit. But how can it be that a sign already made manifest in the pagan land of Nazareth could then be given, as Isaiah prophesied, to the house   *Matthew 1:19* of David? How could God manage to make it happen that the virgin, after accepting the Holy Spirit in her womb, and after remaining for three months in the house of her relative, and after remaining nearly the rest of her pregnancy in Nazareth, not thinking of any journey or any move—how could she then give birth to the Ruler in Israel, according to the prophecy of Micah, in Bethlehem?

Truly here is, as Isaiah himself suggests, a weariness to God Himself. In other words, God planned to enact difficult and inconceivable acts (at least from a human perspective), so that the prophesied sign would occur in the proper place. And so, He chose a universal census for the Virgin Mary (who was accepted finally into the house of Joseph according to the Angel's word) to finally be brought from Nazareth to Bethlehem, thereby to show her Son being a true and triumphant descendant of David. But since censuses were not common among the people of God (it was even prohibited by law), then it was necessary to place the people of God into the authority of another nation. And so, God made nearly all the kingdoms of the Earth tremble and fall before the might of Rome; over Rome He placed Augustus; to Augustus He gave universal peace, so that his might and comfort might suggest to him the thought of census, and so that from him might come the *decree... that all the world should be registered* before the virgin's allotted time for giving birth came about.

This census, seemingly suddenly, but equally inevitably, drew Joseph to his ancestral city of Bethlehem. Mary had to follow Joseph, and the earthly ancestry of Emmanuel was revealed at the same time as His birth. And so, an event that not many days before seemed impossible occurred—He was born exactly as the Prophet predicted, in Bethlehem.

Truly, everything was done in order for the prophecy to be fulfilled, and so that through both small and great deeds of men, the one great sign of God's mastery over human works would be evident. *So all this was done that it might be fulfilled which was spoken*

SERMON 5: ON THE THE NATIVITY, 1824

by the Lord through the Prophet, saying, 'Behold, the virgin shall be with child, and bear a Son, and they shall call His name 'Emmanuel,' which is translated, 'God with us.'

Matthew 1:22-23

While we discuss this exact fulfillment of the prophetic words referring to the birth of our Lord Jesus Christ, someone may ask: "Why was the prophecy concerning His name (Emmanuel) not fulfilled as exactly as the rest of the events? Why did the Angel command Him to be named "Jesus"?

I answer to this first of all in the following manner: if all the other prophesied details concerning the Son of the Virgin came true, including those that seem less significant, such as the place of His birth, then is it at all possible that the Creator of Prophecy, the Holy Spirit, allowed the essence, spirit, and purpose of all lesser details—that is, that the Son of the Virgin brings us close to God in order to save us—to be fulfilled without exactness? Of course not.

Secondly, I admit that there seems on the surface to be something inexact in the combination of the prophecy concerning the name Emmanuel with the event of His birth. But at the same time, I also confidently insist that this apparent inexactness is not only not a deficiency in the prophecy or in the event itself, but actually belongs to the perfection of both, and reveals the divine origin of both in a new, unexpected way. First of all, consider that Emmanuel was both foretold and came to Earth according to the prophecies for the sake of the faithful. Furthermore, wherever there is faith, there must be some measure of obscurity and hiddenness, since faith, according to Apostle Paul, *is the evidence of things not seen*, while a complete and revealed vision would leave no place for faith, only certainty. Therefore, you must agree that Emmanuel, in His coming to Earth, must have been visible enough for Him to be recognized, but hidden enough for faith in Him to be possible. Those who did not believe in Him would not be able to pierce His mysteries, thereby harming the works

Hebrews 11:1

of God, which He was supposed to accomplish. Therefore, that which the Prophet reveals to the faithful in the strange name of Emmanuel is the same thing that the Angel offered to the world under the cover of the not-quite-unusual (for Jewish ears) name of Jesus, for it was a name of one of their Judges and one of their High Priests. The symbolism of this name, then, was not without mystery for the faithful, but it was also hidden from those who did not believe.

Thirdly, if we, not limiting ourselves only to the superficial, but using the help of faith or mystical sight into the invisible, compare the prophetic name of Emmanuel with the historical name of Jesus, then it is not difficult to see in them not only an exact, mutual internal consistency, but even unity. What prevents us people from a reality of *God with us? Your iniquities have separated you from God*. And so, the separation from God, and our sinful state—they are one and the same. Consequently, coming close to God and being saved from sins—they are one and the same. And thus, Emmanuel— *God with us* —and Jesus— *the salvation from sins*—they are one and the same. The prophecy is exact, and the event is truly according to the prophecy. Emmanuel is Savior; Jesus is *God with us*.

Isaiah 59:2

Let us understand, O Christians, the profound wisdom of this prophecy, and let us feel the exalted blessedness of this event! God is with us in Jesus, by the incarnation, since in Him, divinity and humanity not only come close, but are united inseparably, without any division, into the single hypostasis of the God-man. Thus, "He is not ashamed to call [us] brethren" (Hebrews 2:11).

God is with us in Jesus, by the Atonement, since without Jesus sin would still be with us, for we inherited sin from Adam, and we ourselves did not cease to continue in it. And *whoever commits sin is a slave of sin*. It used to be that the devil was with us, for *He who sins is of the devil*. However, Jesus, having come to Earth, fulfilled the Law of God by His life, though we had transgressed the Law; by His sufferings, He blotted out the sins that we had

John 8:34
1 John 3:8

committed; by His death, He put death to death, even though we were condemned to death for our sins. By His descent into Hell, He freed us from the dark power of the devil; by His Resurrection, He once again found *the life of God* for us, even though we were *alienated from* it. *Ephesians 4:18*

God is with us in Jesus, by the gift of the Holy Spirit, since the Son of God, who came into the world to redeem us, returned to Heaven, that He might *pray the Father, and He will give [us] another Helper, that He may abide with [us] forever.* *John 14:16*

God is with us through Jesus, in our mind and understanding, since *no one has seen God at any time. The only begotten Son, who is in the bosom of the Father, He has declared Him.* *John 1:18*

God is with us through Jesus, in our hearts and emotions, since *Christ [dwells] in [our] hearts through faith*, and at the same time *the love of God [pours] out in our hearts by the Holy Spirit who was given to us.* *Ephesians 3:17*

Romans 5:5

God is with us through Jesus, in all our life and deeds, if only we completely commit ourselves to Him, since then *it is no longer [we] who live, but Christ lives in [us]* and *God... works in [us] both to will and to do for His good pleasure.* *Galatians 2:20*

Philippians 2:13

God is with us through Jesus, if only we desire it, in all circumstances and events of our life; so that even when we suffer, we may suffer together with Him, *that we may also be glorified together.* If we die, *we die to the Lord.* *Romans 8:17; 14:8*

In the name of our Lord Jesus Christ, God is with us, O Christians, always in all things! Only let us not cease to be with God, through remembrance of Him, through prayer to Him, through faith and love, through constantly laboring in those things that please Him and that bring us close to Him. Amen.

6

Homily on the Nativity of Christ (1826)

> *Let this mind be in you which was also in Christ Jesus,*
> *who, being in the form of God, did not consider it robbery*
> *to be equal with God, but made Himself of no reputation,*
> *taking the form of a bondservant, and coming*
> *in the likeness of men (Philippians 2:5-7).*

If, according to Solomon, *To everything there is a season, a time for every purpose under Heaven,* then is not today the time to contemplate with love, together with the Apostle, the miraculous kenosis of our great God and Savior Jesus Christ, when we see Him reduced to the size of a human child, having humbled Himself to lay in a manger?

Ecclesiastes 3:18

People who are passionately attached to earthly greatness are often upset by the humility of Jesus Christ. However, after the experience of so many centuries, it is clear that *God also has highly exalted Him,* so highly in fact that truly *at the name of Jesus every knee [bows] of those in Heaven, and of those on Earth, and of those under the Earth.* For, from the day of His Resurrection and Ascension, thousands of witnesses have seen how the heavenly hosts ful-

Philippians 2:9-10

filled all His commands, while the powers of Hell on the contrary were cast down into the abyss. As for humanity, millions find their blessedness in worshiping Him. After accounting for all this, especially since we are gathered before people who have come together to bow at the name of Jesus, we can free ourselves from the burden of protecting or justifying His humiliation. Thus, no one will prevent us from looking at His kenosis with the same veneration as we look at His greatness.

Oh, how great was the self-emptying of the Son of God in His incarnation! This lessening must be all the more striking to us, since it is a kind of polar opposite to the original glorification of man himself. For the word of God, not without purpose, uses the same expression for both of these opposites: image and likeness. God the Creator said, *Let Us make man in Our image, according to Our likeness*. And the Apostle said, concerning the incarnation of the Son of God, *[He] made Himself of no reputation, taking the form of a bondservant, and coming in the likeness of men*. For any other lord, it does not take much self-lessening to appear in the form of a servant. However, when the great and exalted Lord, who gives even His slaves the image of lordship, appears Himself in the "image and likeness" of a slave, that is, in the actual state of complete slavery, and profound humiliation, as is typical of slavery, then we cannot fail to look at such self-lessening with a profound sense of wonder that either grows to compunction or to terror. This is how the Son of God lessened Himself in the incarnation.

Genesis 1:26

Philippians 2:5-7

But He humbled Himself far more in the circumstances of His earthly birth! He had to choose a nation into which He would be born. And He chose of all nations on the Earth the smallest, one that had no form of self-government, one that had many times been enslaved and was near yet another enslavement, and one that had once been blessed but was on the verge now of being rejected completely. He needed to choose a city, and He chose Bethlehem, which was so insignificant that even the well-intentioned Prophet could not hide his censure and could find no other way of glorifying it than by the name of the humiliated Jesus, who was to be born in it: *But you, Bethlehem Ephrathah, though you are little among the thousands of Judah, yet out of you shall come forth to Me, the One to be Ruler in Israel, whose going forth is from of old, from everlasting.*

<small>Micah 5:2</small>

He had to choose a mother. Furthermore, in order to conceal the mystery of the incarnation from unbelievers until the proper time, He also had to be tied to an apparent father by the ties of the Law (though not the flesh). And so He chose them, and though they were descendants of kings (necessary for the promise and the prophecy to be fulfilled), the one was a simple carpenter, and the other a poor, orphaned virgin. And what else? If the Lord had been born in the small dwelling of Joseph (whether owned or rented), and if Mary had put Him into a poor cradle, the image of the slave that He took upon Himself perhaps would not have included all the elements that it could, for one could easily find a slave-hut smaller than Joseph's, or a cradle poorer than Mary's. And so what does the infinitely Great One do in His search for endless kenosis? Through Augustus' command that the entire world (cosmos) be counted in census, He brings into movement the entire population of the land of Judea, so much so that Joseph could not either remain in his own home in Nazareth, nor find a rented home in Bethlehem when it came time for the true Lord of the cosmos to be born. And so, the One who lessened Himself even to human childhood lowers Himself still further, even to having a manger instead of a cradle. *[She] laid Him in a manger, because there was no room for them in the inn.*

<small>Luke 2:1</small>

<small>Luke 2:7</small>

If we extend our gaze from the self-emptying God to the entire expanse of the world for whose sake He humbled Himself, the miracle of kenosis will offer even more astounding realities for our vision. Here it comes to my mind how the Word of God descended from the heavens to the land of Egypt, as described by the writer of the book of Wisdom: *For while gentle silence embraced everything and night at its own speed was half over, Your all-power-*

SERMON 6: ON THE THE NATIVITY OF CHRIST, 1826

ful Word leaped from Heaven, from the royal throne, into the midst of a doomed land, a relentless warrior carrying the sharp sword of Your irrevocable command. Didn't it also happen that during the descent of the incarnate Word of God into the land of Israel, halfway through the night, at the very moment of His birth, *there were in the same country shepherds living out in the fields, keeping watch over their flocks by night?* Was not the entire world gripped in gentle silence when only the voice of the Angel was heard, and heard only by a small crowd of shepherds in the desert? *Wis. of Sol. 18:14-15*
Luke 2:8

What a horrifying obscurity served as the background for the descent of the avenging Word of God down to the perishing land of Egypt to *fill all things with death* through striking down of all the firstborn of Egypt! It should be said that this obscurity not only did not lessen, but only increased the glory of the Avenger-God, who used only His silent command to dim the light of life of the impure ones, without any visible means, without any perceptible actions. Different, but no less terrifying, was the obscurity in which the saving Word of God, being born in the flesh, came to visit the whole world, which was perishing because the earthborn *all have sinned and fallen short of the glory of God.* He came, but not like a frightening warrior that threatened death to all that lived, but as a newborn baby, who brought the hope of rebirth and life to the region of death. *Wis. of Sol. 18:16*
Romans 3:23

He comes, but the dying Earth does not meet Him, it does not embrace Him, it does not glorify Him, it does not even see its Savior or hear the Word of God who lies silently in the manger. It is almost as though in vain did Jesus have glory from God the Father *before the world was*, and this glory is only heard in the mouths of the Angels that follow Him down into the world. On this fading world, there are almost no ears that are not deafened by the cares of the world, none that are capable of hearing the glory of the Angels. It is almost in vain that the wisest and most well-known of all the stars performs an incredible journey to *John 17:5* show that the Sun of righteousness is shining through the darkest night. There are hardly two or three people capable of recognizing this miracle and then being ready to follow it, and they are those who sit in the darkness and the shadow of paganism and celestial worship!

Where is Judah, the place where *God is known?* Judea does not know that *God was manifested in the flesh.* What about Jerusalem, the *city of God?* It is not participating in the Joy of Christ who came to save, but it is disturbed together with Herod, who seeks to kill Him. And what about the High Priests and scribes who were supposed to be especially close to God and His mysteries through prayer and knowledge of the Law? They were very good at answering the scholarly question of *where the Christ was to be born*, and they are so pleased with themselves that they don't consider it necessary to know whether or not He has actually been born. And so, it was not only in the natural midnight of time, but more so in the profound night of ignorance and forgetfulness of God and His judgments, that *Your all-powerful Word leaped from Heaven, from the royal throne, into the midst of a doomed land.* In spite of the fact that nearly no one glorified Him, no one knew Him or even tried to come to know Him, He does not utter any rebuking words. Instead, He remains silent in long-suffering, so salvific for the doomed! And so, He who was equal to God, God Himself, diminished Himself, but He did even more than that — He assumed a double humiliation from the ignorance and lack of care of those for love of whom He humbled Himself!

Psalm 75:2
1 Timothy 3:16
Psalm 86:3

Matthew 2:4

(Wis. of Sol. 18:15)

Let us wonder, O Christians, at this willing kenosis of our great God and Savior, but this is not enough. We must also reverence this kenosis, but even that is not enough. *Let this mind be in you which was also in Christ Jesus.* You must have the same disposition as Jesus Christ Himself had. What does that mean? The Apostle Paul explains: *Let nothing be done through selfish ambition or conceit, but in lowliness of mind let each esteem others better than himself.* From this, it becomes evident that he teaches us to emulate Jesus Christ in not rating ourselves highly, in not puffing

Philippians 2:5

Philippians 2:3

ourselves up over others, but in humbling ourselves within ourselves and before others.

Whoever lives in a magnificent house, sleeps on goose down, and dresses in silks — remember the cave and the manger, and with them the rough swaddling clothes of our Savior. Having remembered, let us not humiliate those who live in poor houses, sleep on straw, wear rough clothing, and who, perhaps, are not only externally similar to Christ, but who also have His disposition. *Let the rich glory in his humiliation.* *Paraphrase of James 1:10*

And whoever, according to the expression of the Apostle, *rest[s] on the Law, and make[s] [his] boast in God, and know[s] His will, and approve[s] the things that are excellent, being instructed out of the Law,* let him *who glories, let him glory in the Lord! Therefore let him who thinks he stands take heed lest he fall.* Let him especially not condemn the ignorant or laugh at those who fall! Christ is "the true Light which gives light to every man coming into the world" (John 1:9). Perhaps the person whom we see sitting in the valley and the shadow of death will be illumined by that light more quickly than you, or perhaps he is already shining inside, in the realm of the spirit. Perhaps the wise men of the pagan East seek Christ more zealously than you, and perhaps they will find Him before you. Perhaps *tax collectors and harlots enter the Kingdom of God before you.* *Romans 2:17-18; 1 Corinthians 1:31, 10:12*

Matthew 21:31

Meekness, simplicity, humility, compassion to the poor, making yourself equal with those below you, calmness in humiliation, and patience that cannot be defeated by any insults: *Let this mind be in you,* as it was *also in Christ Jesus.* Amen. *Philippians 2:5-7*

Homily on the day of the Nativity of Christ (1834)

*Then the Angel said to them,
'Do not be afraid, for behold, I bring you good tidings
of great joy which will be to all people. For there is born to you
this day in the city of David a Savior, who is Christ the Lord
(Luke 2:10-11).*

Luke 2:10
Luke 2:10

What joy does the Angel give to the shepherds of Bethlehem! Truly, they are *tidings of great joy*. And truly, as he predicted, this joy *will be to all people*. And so, after the fulfillment of all that has been prophesied, this joy, without a doubt, belongs also to you who stand here, and to all the people of God, from the least to the greatest, to all who will not close the eye of their mind to come to know that truth, who will not harden their hearts to feel that joy.

Luke 2:11

What sort of joy is this? The Angel explains: *For there is born to you this day...* I interrupt the words of the messenger to show you the beginning of the joy at the very inception of his message. Birth is always more or less joyful, because it represents the growth and triumph of life, and because, on the contrary, death is always more or less sad, since having swallowed up one life, it always threatens the same to all those who remain alive. Birth is especially joyful to those who have just had their child born. If he is born to a well-known family, this is a joy to that family. If he is born also for his people and government, such as a king's son, especially an heir, then this joy belongs to the entire nation and people.

The Angel said, *to you is born…* To whom? Was he then born only for the shepherds of Bethlehem who heard the word of the Angel? But the Angel said that the joy would belong to all people; this shows that through the shepherds, he is looking at all people. This is why he announced this joy as belonging *to all people*. This child is born for you, for all people, not a single family or nation, but for all mankind on Earth, for all who were, who are, and who yet will be. What an incredible joy! Now you can, each of you, rejoice for yourselves and for the entire human race, for those who have lived out their days and left to eternity, whom you remember with sadness, or do not know how to remember them, and for all your descendants as well, for whom, perhaps, you do care a great deal.

Luke 2:11

Luke 2:10

Let us ask for further elucidation from the Angel: why must this announced birth bring universal joy? He says, *For there is born to you this day in the city of David a Savior.* In the history of the people of God, we have seen many famous men who have been the instruments of God's salvation. *And when the Lord raised up judges for them, the Lord was with the judge and delivered them out of the hand of their enemies all the days of the judge.* It also happened before that this salvation was announced by an Angel, as occurred with Gideon: *Go in this might of yours, and you shall save Israel from the hand of the Midianites.* But these temporary and partial salvations could not be the source of joy for all people, because they did not extend to all people, and quickly they would give way to yet another evil and calamity. *And it came to pass, when the judge*

Luke 2:11

Judges 2:18

Judges 6:14

was dead, *that they reverted and behaved more corruptly than their fathers*. But now is born the Savior of all people, a true Savior who was only weakly prefigured by all the famous men of power and salvation in the Old Testament histories. He is a universal Savior, whose salvation reaches out to all, to whomever does not desire to destroy himself willingly, that is. He is a Savior for all times, and no new calamity dares attack those whom He saves.

The messenger of joy adds more explanation: *For there is born to you this day in the city of David a Savior, who is Christ the Lord*. It seems that the shepherds of Bethlehem already had some understanding of the coming Savior, since the heavenly messenger, seeing their thoughts, thought it enough to give them the great news of joy, saying only that the Promised One is the Christ. And truly, it would have been impossible for the shepherds to avoid hearing the words of the Psalter in the Temple: *The Lord has saved His Christ*, and in another place: *The Lord is the strength of His people, and He is the defender of the salvation of His anointed (that is, His Christ)*.

These Psalm verses tell us a good deal about the nature of the Angel's declaration of a sign to the shepherds. The Psalms offer an image of a Christ who needs to be saved first, before becoming the salvation of others. However, in the words of the Angel, the Christ is the Savior, and He needs no one to save Him, for He has the power to save in His own essence, and He acts on that power without limit: *A Savior, who is Christ the Lord*. The Psalmist seems only to come to a new knowledge when he finds out that the Lord favors, protects, and saves the Christ: Now *know I that the Lord hath saved His Christ*. The Angel, however, announces a Christ who is the Lord Himself (that is, an anointed one of God) whom God has anointed, as another Prophet said: *The Lord has anointed Me to preach good tidings to the poor; He has sent Me to heal the brokenhearted, to proclaim liberty to the captives, and the opening of the prison to those who are bound; to proclaim the acceptable year of the*

Lord, and the day of vengeance of our God; to comfort all who mourn, to console those who mourn in Zion, to give them beauty for ashes, the oil of joy for mourning, the garment of praise for the spirit of heaviness. How- *Isaiah 61:1-3* ever, this same Anointed One is also the Lord God, who Himself has the power not only to save those who are threatened by destruction, but even to save those who have already perished, to raise the dead, to justify the condemned, to bless those under the curse of breaking the Law, to transform the slaves of Hell into the children of God.

O what limitless joy, reaching from Heaven to Hell, as greatly desired as salvation, as sweet and lovely as the anointing of the Spirit of God, as mighty as the Lord who is the source of it! I would fall silent now, because even this is enough to feel it, since it is also true that no word is sufficient to fully express it.

But the message of the Angel has not finished. Let us hear it to the end. He also wanted to show a sign, a tangible proof that would better help them understand the joy, to become the more fully established in it: *And this will be the sign to you.* What sign? Where is it? Show it to us. Here it is: *You will find a Babe wrapped in swaddling clothes, lying in a manger.* *Luke 2:12*

Oh, messenger of joy! Have you not destroyed that joy, thinking to make it more exalted and to confirm it with a sign? What sort of joy is it to see a child not wrapped in porphyry or fine linens, not in a bridal chamber or a brightly lit house, not even in a hut, not even in a cradle, because no hut or cradle was found for Him, but in a manger! Consequently, He must be in some haven for speechless beasts, or in a deserted place not even protected from the night wind of December. Does not such a sign make people pity the birth-giver and the Child, or even make them fear for His life, instead of giving them joy? But we must not think that the messenger of Heaven came to delude the Earth through a false promise, or through a delusive sign of joy. If we who are born on Earth do not see his words as a sign of joy, then is it not because we do not see with the pure, heavenly eye, which sees things more clearly than our earthly eyes, which have not yet been purified from the dust of vanity?

"Let us purify our eyes and see," as the canon of Pascha reminds us. Let us purify our mind, let us come to know the mystery of Christ the Lord, and let us purify our hearts and be sweetened by His joy, in spite of the external appearance of sorrow. Having thought about it more deeply, I begin to understand the Angel, and I admit that the incomparable sight of a Child wrapped in swaddling clothes and lying in a manger is truly a sign, not so much of extreme need and poverty as of incomparable joy. For tell me, in what other form would you like to find the Christ who was born here, our Lord and Savior? Would you prefer to see Him in heavenly glory, proper to Him as Lord? But before this glory the Cherubim tremble, and they close their eyes before it. Or what about earthly glory? But would this be a sight more joyful than the simple swaddling clothes and the humble manger? Do many people have access to earthly glory? And is it anything other than superficial glister? Those who look at that brilliance, for the most part, have no way of reaching it, and those from whom the brilliance comes forth know that earthly glory is not the most trustworthy sign of joy.

No! Let us cease to look for signs of joy through our own brazen perspective, for it is not trustworthy. Let us plunge more deeply into the sign that is given to us. Why do we need a sign of joy? Because we do not have enough joy. Why do we need the Savior, Christ the Lord? Because we fear perdition. Why is our joy insufficient? Why do we fear perdition? Because we are far from the life of God; because we live in the corruption of sin. And if that is the case, then is it not a good sign that the Savior who was born for our sake begins to show himself exactly in the place where the first punishment for sin was endured, according to the words of the Judge: *In pain you shall bring forth children*?

Genesis 3:16

As a wise physician, He approaches the very source and root of our sickness, of our sinful corruption with His healing, divine power. What other sign could be more desirable to the one who seeks healing? Because of this profound and all-wise beginning, it is not difficult to conclude what perfect medicine He is preparing. It is also not insignificant that, having lowered Himself to such a humble birth, He lowers Himself still more to the humiliation of the manger. Through this, He gives us a special sign that, though sin might humiliate you even to the level of bestial passions and desires, even if you are forced to turn the prophetic rebuke against yourself—*But man, being in honor, understood it not; he shall be compared unto the brute beasts, and is become like unto them*—even then, you should not despair of the compassion of your Savior, who, not having considered it unworthy to lie in a manger, would not also consider it beneath His dignity to place His grace and His peace in the manger of your soul if only you fall down before Him in repentance and faith. *Psalm 48:13*

And so, *Come to me, all you who labor and are heavy laden* with sins, misfortunes, pain of conscience, fear of eternal judgment and perdition. Behold, here is the sign of your salvation and, consequently, your joy—all the joy you could ever desire. Here is the sign: *You will find a Babe wrapped in swaddling clothes, lying in a manger, who is Christ the Lord.* *Matthew 11:28*

Luke 2:11

Approach therefore the Savior-Child, and be like children through your lack of malice and your meekness. Approach the Swaddled One, and tie up your sinful self-will. Give up your will to the will of your Savior. Approach the one lying in the manger, and reveal your impure, bestial life, and instead of it, establish a spiritual life. Approach the silent Word with silent groaning of your constantly praying heart, and God the Word will speak His unutterable joy into your hearts. Then you will come to know the heavenly messenger of joy; then you will cry out, with the mother who gave birth to Christ: *My soul magnifies the Lord, and my spirit has rejoiced in God my savior.* Amen. *Luke 1:46-47*

8

Homily on the Transfiguration (1820)

[They] went up on the mountain to pray. As He prayed, the appearance of His face was altered, and His robe become white and glistening. And behold, two men talked with Him, who were Moses and Elijah (Luke 9:38-30).

What an exalted spectacle occurred on Mount Tabor! A spectacle truly worthy of being looked at with joy, as the Apostles did, and of being remembered with triumph, as we do today. It was no accident that those who were witnesses of the great manifestations at Sinai and Horeb—Moses and Elijah—appeared on Tabor. What they saw on Tabor was even more spectacular than what they saw in their own lives. On Sinai and Horeb the power and glory of God revealed itself to mankind through visible matter, but on Tabor not only did divinity appear to man, but human nature itself appeared in divine glory. Moses shook with fear on Sinai; Elijah complained on Horeb. For the Apostles on Tabor, joy shone through their terror: *Lord, it is good for us to be here.*

Hebrews 12:21
3 Kingdoms 29:14
Matthew 17:4

O Christians! Truly, your hearts must be ready to say concerning those who witnessed the glory on Tabor: Truly it was good for them to be there! How fortunate were they that they could have been there! But what if I were to tell you that the path to the contemplation of Tabor's glory is not swallowed by the abyss of time, is not blocked by a wall, is not overgrown with thorns, not forgotten or lost, but is to this day revealed, by those who are cognizant of it, to those who desire it? It's not difficult to understand that what I speak of is a spiritual journey, for of course, no physical journey is possible to scale the heights of spiritual visions and divine revelations. In actual fact, why did the evangelist, when beginning to describe the glorious Transfiguration of the Lord, begin by focusing our attention on prayer? "[They] went up on the mountain to pray." Why indeed, except that it seems that he does not trust the perspicacity of certain readers of the Gospel and fears that they might not fully understand the importance of this fact, and so he immediately repeats that the Transfiguration of the Lord occurred during prayer: *As He prayed.* Why else would he do this if not to show us that in prayer itself is the path toward the light of Tabor, the key to spiritual mysteries and the power of divine revelations?

If the wisest evangelist found it so necessary to connect the vision of the glory of Tabor with the thoughts of prayer, then of course it would be remiss of us Christians not to connect our remembrance of this wondrous feast day with some short thoughts concerning the power and action of prayer.

Even though we must hope that in this house of prayer there is no one who doesn't have at least some knowledge of the power and action of prayer, however, for more complete knowledge, it is permissible to enter this examination with the assumption that we are describing something unknown. And so, does a particular kind of prayer have a particular kind of effect? This question cannot long remain unanswered. It is answered by the general knowledge of the human race, for everyone--from the

Christian, who is enlightened by pure faith, to the pagan, who is darkened by crude superstition—all people admit that prayer is a necessity, and the greater and better part of mankind perform this duty of prayer in actual fact, though not all in the same manner or with the same effectiveness. But what would be the point of praying at all, if we didn't admit that it had power or if we didn't expect it to have any effect?

If anyone asks how the pagans could have been witnesses to the power of prayer when they had no true worship of God or true prayer, then we will answer with another question: how do they have any kind of prayer at all? No matter how you try to explain it away, even if you admit it is an incomplete form of prayer, you can't avoid the reality that the source of its appearance in the first place must be the power of prayer.

Even pagans pray, naturally, for one of several reasons. Either God, although His creation has abandoned Him, has not abandoned His creation, leaving in the pagan's darkened heart some sparks of His light, which *gives light to every man coming into the world*, that the darkness cannot comprehend, which even in the flesh arouses a certain sense of spiritual hunger, gives a certain foretaste of the possibility of that hunger's being filled, and in this manner inspires the pagan to cry out to the unknown God for unknown help. Or, it is possible that even in the swamp of sensuality that soils paganism, sometimes certain inspired souls appeared who, acknowledging the baseness and impurity of this state, reached a certain level of communion with the powers of the spiritual world through a sincere desire and effort to know them. And then, they began to teach others to achieve the same through sincere and firm desire, that is, through prayer. Finally, it is possible that since the times when a true knowledge of God had spread to the entire human race, when the whole world knew well the power and efficacy of true prayer, in spite of the subsequent loss of true worship, some indelible universal assurance

(margin: John 1:9; John 1:5)

remained both of the necessity of the worship of God Himself, and of the usefulness of prayer, that is, its power and efficacy.

Unfortunately, there is a philosophy of the kind that the Apostle Paul calls *according to the basic principles of the world, and not according to Christ* that, ignoring the witness of the human race completely, ascribes the most hopeful witness to the truth to its own self. Such a philosophy teaches that the whole world is interconnected by a series of causes and effects, in which all free beings are more or less entangled. Let's say a person prays, for example, for a bountiful harvest. This harvest depends on good weather, while the good weather depends on the interaction of sun, earth, and water, while their activity depends on the laws of nature, which were once established by the Creator and subsequently continued to act constantly and inevitably. Thus, the person who prays for a bountiful harvest either wastes his time or does it only for the sake of his own humility and submission before the power and majesty of the Creator.

Colossians 2:8

Let us note that even such a way of thinking cannot deprive prayer of at least the power to form within man the quality of humility before God—this is no small thing. However, it is not enough. Ask, if you meet one of the postulants of this wisdom, what is better: an automated machine or a living, free, reasoning creature, and a prosperous society of such free beings? What is more exalted: an artist who built an automaton and watches it move, or a father who gave birth to children, and by raising them properly, forms in them his own likeness? Or a king who founded a kingdom of free creatures and rules over them just as they wish to be guided, except without the transgression of his all-wise and good intentions? This is not a difficult choice, and we shouldn't even wait long for an answer.

Ask them something else: why do they prefer to see a completed composition in the creation of the all-perfect Creator, instead of a well-established kingdom of a wise King and a great mansion of the all-good Father? Why do they prefer to imagine God as an Artist of the world, instead of the King of Heaven and Earth and the Father of spirits? Let us offer them to seek the answer to these questions in their own consciences, but for our present purposes, it is enough to say that if God is not only our Creator, but also our Father and King, then there can be no doubt that the children do not call on their Father in vain, nor do the sons of the Kingdom cry out to a King who has stopped His ears.

Is it so strange if a loving Father stops or at least changes the movement of a machine that He has built to fulfill a good, or at least innocent, desire of His son? Just so, it is not at all strange if the all-good heavenly Father, according to the prayers of His earth-born children, gives a new, unexpected direction to nature, though it be governed by a law of inevitability? This is how Truth Himself explains the action of prayer: *If you then, being evil, know how to give good gifts to your children, how much more will your Father who is in Heaven give good things to those who ask Him!*

<small>Matthew 7:11</small>

Some Christians, who perform the work of prayer externally, more as a matter of ritual than as an internal reality of the spirit, do not doubt the indefinite concept that prayer can be powerful and effective. However, they are either confused or completely wrong about the application of this general thought to their own prayer life. Though they pray often, they see no perceptible effects to their prayer either in themselves or around them, and instead of doubting the truthfulness or worth of their own prayers, they are inspired by a spirit of laziness and self-delusion to believe that powerful or effective prayer is, perhaps, only a special gift of grace, given to some chosen ones of God, only in certain extraordinary circumstances.

To such people we answer without a moment's hesitation: there is no person whose prayer cannot become powerful if he desires it firmly and with a pure heart, with faith and hope in God. And there is no situation in which prayer cannot become effective, if only the object of prayer is not contrary to the wisdom and goodness of God or the benefit of the one praying. We have said as much already. However, we hope that we are not deluding those who truly love prayer.

Imagine a man who can turn the rain on and off with the power of his prayer. He commands that a handful of flour and a bit of oil be enough to feed several people for a few months, or maybe even a whole year, and all this actually happens! He breathes on a dead body, and it resurrects. He calls fire from Heaven to consume an altar table and offering that have been soaked with water. What is more extraordinary than such power of prayer? But it only seems thus to a person who doesn't know spiritual power; while the one who knows sees these events as normal. This is not my own opinion, but apostolic teaching.

The Apostle James, who taught us to pray for one another, confirms this command by saying that *the effective, fervent prayer of a righteous man avails much*. Both the command and the confirming saying he proves by the example of the same extraordinary person whom we have already described and whom he called a man like unto us: *Elijah was a man with a nature like ours, and he prayed earnestly that it would not rain; and it did not rain on the land for three years and six months. And he prayed again, and the heavens gave rain, and the Earth produced its fruit.* Why did James say that Elijah "was a man with a nature like ours"? Exactly for this reason: so that, as you consider him to be a typical human being, you do not fail to emulate him and acquire strength through prayer.

James 5:16

James 5:16-18

In spite of this, emulating the prayer of the Prophet might seem to us a labor beyond our abilities, a height unscalable to our weakness. If that is the case, then imagine yourselves as whatever you like—less than the Prophet, or even less than Christian, or even no better than a pagan! Even in this case, I insist that your prayer can be strong and effective. It can make you true Christians, even if you are only pagans. It can even lead you to true knowledge of God and true worship of God, even if such a thing is unknown to you, or even if there is no person near you who might lead you to it. Prayer itself will open Heaven for you and send down an Angel from there, who will instruct you personally.

But am I perhaps imagining things, carried away with a desire to inspire you to active and powerful prayer? No, dear brothers and fellow laborers in prayer, I am only speaking of things that have already happened, and so can happen again, as witnessed by our sacred books. Take, for example, the centurion Cornelius from the Book of Acts, who was a pagan. It is not clear whether or not he knew the one God, but it is clear that he did not know *Jesus Christ whom [God] had sent*. However, he did as much good as he knew how to do. He feared and constantly called upon God, even if he did not know Him: *a devout man and one who feared God with all his household, who gave alms generously to the people, and prayed to God always*. And what did this constant prayer of the pagan accomplish? It literally brought the heavens down to him, calling down heavenly, even divine, powers. In the middle of his prayer, an Angel appeared to him. *Cornelius*, said the Angel, *your prayer has been heard, and your alms are remembered in the sight of God*. Then the Angel taught him to call on the Apostle Peter. When the Apostle preached Jesus Christ to him, the Holy Spirit, even before baptism, poured His grace on Cornelius.

If you want, try to imagine something that seems impossible to achieve with the power of prayer. Still, I do not despair of being able, through the light of the Word of God, to show you that even this thing is possible and achievable, even if it seems impossible. Imagine, for example, an entire nation that had irritated God with a serious transgression; add to that, that God already uttered His holy will to destroy this nation, and in these horrifying minutes there was literally only one person on Earth who could offer a prayer for this people, though they were in the midst of being swallowed by Hell itself!

Does it not seem to you that such a nation was beyond help? And yet, Moses's experience proves the opposite. The nation of Israel, immediately after the glorious revelation of God and the giving of the tablets of the Law on Sinai, suddenly turned to idolatry. Moses stood before God on the mountain. Listen and understand what extraordinary words the Lord uttered to Moses at this moment: *Let Me alone, that My wrath may burn hot against them and I may consume them.* O Lord of spirits and of all flesh! Can this slave of Yours, who is only powerful through Your power, contradict the fulfillment of Your will? Leave Me, He said, I want to reveal My righteous anger; I want to destroy this nation; but you are preventing Me. *Let Me alone, that My wrath may burn hot against them and I may consume them.* And what else? The holy man doesn't leave God even then, but instead he increases his prayer, and the anger of the invincible Almighty fades away before the power of a mortal man's prayer. *So the Lord relented from the harm which He said He would do to His people.* Measure, if you can, the miraculous power of prayer in this case, and you will see that there is nothing it cannot accomplish for salvation!

Exodus 32:10

Exodus 32:10

Exodus 32:14

In order to further see how easily the key of prayer can open spiritual and divine treasures, let us look up again at Tabor, which we tried to approach with today's reflections. Let us look intently again at the way the evangelist describes the Transfiguration of the Lord: *[They] went up on the mountain to pray. As He prayed, the appearance of His face was altered, and His robe become white and glistening. And behold, two men talked with Him, who were Moses and Elijah.* If we dare to guess, based only on these words, the divine mystery of the heart of Jesus, it seems to us that on the way to Tabor, His immediate intention was not Transfiguration at all, but simply prayer. It seems to us that on that very mountain, in the very moments of the Transfiguration, His intention was only to pray. It may not seem impossible to guess that the object of this prayer of the Savior was His preparation of Himself and His disciples for the coming suffering and death on the Cross, which He had not long before revealed to His disciples, and concerning which He spoke with Moses and Elijah during the Transfiguration itself.

Luke 9:38-30

Luke 9:22

Luke 9:31

How then did the glory reveal itself in the middle of a prayer concerning imminent suffering? It was like a self-generating flower, a fruit of the abundant, living power of prayer. The spirit of prayer, combining with the Spirit of God, filled the soul of Jesus with light; the excess of that light, unable to be contained in the soul, poured out onto the body, and His face shone. The light was unable to be contained even there, and it shone on and transformed even His clothing, and going out even further, it filled the souls of the Apostles and was reflected in Peter's exclamation: *It is good for us to be here!* It then passed into the region of the inner world, and it pulled Moses and Elijah from there. It reached the very bosom of the heavenly Father and inspired His love toward a triumphant witness concerning His beloved: *This is My beloved Son, in whom I am well pleased. Hear Him!*

Matthew 17:4

Matthew 17:5

O the miracle of prayer, which united in a single action Heaven and Earth and the Divinity Himself! Let no one say that this example of prayer doesn't refer to us, since it is the work of the God-man. It does refer to us, O Christians; for that which was accomplished in Christ must be accomplished in us also, though not to the same degree: *Let this mind be in you which was also in Christ Jesus.*

Philippians 2:5

Finally, the time has come to ask: why do so many prayers remain unanswered, if every prayer can be so powerful and effective? For we have answered every possible objection. Let us point out one example when a prayer seems to be ineffective, while in actual fact it is answered in an unexpected and exalted fashion. Thus, the Apostle Paul *pleaded with the Lord three times* to be rescued from a *thorn in the flesh*. But the Lord answered instead: *My grace is sufficient for you, for My strength is made perfect in weakness.* The temptation was not removed from him, but he was instead given an even greater victory over the continuing temptation.

2 Corinthians 12:8-9

If we exclude such cases, then all prayers that fail to be heard are explained by this short explanation of the Apostle: *Yet you do not have because you do not ask. You ask and do not receive because you ask amiss, that you may spend it on your pleasures.* Our prayers are fruitless either because our petitions are not persistent or diligent enough, or because they are not coming from the depths of the soul and we do not pour our whole soul into them. Instead, we only utter weak desires without an aroused spirit, and still we think that they should fulfill themselves automatically. Or our petitions themselves are impure or evil, or we ask for something evil, not useful for our soul, or we ask it not for the glory of God but to satiate our carnal or selfish desires.

James 4:2-3

Pray, O Christian, with a strong prayer, with the full strength of your soul, with attentive and persistent prayer, and with good and pure prayer. If you do not find such prayer within yourself, then pray for that kind of prayer, and through prayer you will first find sincere and active prayer, and then together with you it will defeat all evil, and it will find everything for you, leading you up to Tabor, or revealing Tabor within you. It will call Heaven down into your soul, and it will raise your soul to heaven. Amen.

9

Homily on Transfiguration (1826)

Assuredly, I say to you, there are some standing here who shall not taste death till they see the Son of Man coming in His Kingdom (Matthew 16:28).

The Jews, from the days of their forefather Abraham, expected the coming of a certain blessed Kingdom that was supposed to be established through a promised seed, in whom, by the promise, all the nations of the Earth would be blessed. But more than forty generations passed into oblivion after Abraham before the promised seed and the expected Kingdom manifested themselves. Thus, it was very important for them to hear that there were already some people alive who would live to see the coming of the Kingdom.

Assuredly, I say to you, there are some standing here who shall not taste death till they see the Son of Man coming in His Kingdom. O Christians! We do not await an imaginary, blessed earthly kingdom as the Jews did, but we faithfully await the coming of a spiritual Kingdom, the Kingdom of Heaven, the Kingdom of God Himself. However, do not some of us become like the Jews in the sense that we limit the coming of the Kingdom of God to what lies beyond death? Therefore, is this teaching of the Gospel not also new for us, and necessary for us, lest we remain ignorant of a truth long ago pronounced? It is a very important truth: there are and must be people who encounter the Kingdom of God while still alive.

There are some standing here who shall not taste death till they see the Son of Man coming in His Kingdom. The Kingdom of Jesus Christ, the Son of God, is a Kingdom for all ages. The Psalmist wrote about it, and the Apostle Paul interpreted his words concerning the Son of God thus: *Your throne, O God, is forever and ever.* And let no one think that this only refers to eternity in the future, or the endless Kingdom of the Son of God that must come after the end, for that same Apostle Paul, in the same epistle, says, *He made the worlds...and uphold[s] all things by the word of His power.* Consequently, His kingly power is eternal in the full meaning of the word, meaning it has no beginning point in time, nor any end at any point in history. Truly, He rules over creation while creation still exists. Therefore, the Kingdom of the Son of God not only will be, but is, and was. It is not imminent; it abides. It is not bounded by any limitations but stretches out endlessly. *Matthew 16:28*

Hebrews 1:8

Hebrews 1:2-3

So why do the disciples ask the Lord, *Lord, will you at this time restore the kingdom to Israel?*. What is John saying when he preaches the coming of the Kingdom of Heaven? One believes the Kingdom of Heaven to be far away, the others think that the kingdom of Israel, by which they of course meant the Kingdom of Jesus Christ, the Son of God, was not yet established. This might be true of the Kingdom of the Son of God with reference to people, but not to God Himself. *Acts 1:6*

Matthew 3:2

The Kingdom of Heaven is distant, truly, if men do not know it; it is not yet established when people have not yet formed themselves into an instrument of that Kingdom. The Kingdom of Heaven approaches men who come to know it; it is established when *you are being built together for a dwelling place of God in the Spirit*. Since man can only fully experience the Kingdom of Heaven *Ephesians 2:22* in the heavens, the divine reality in God Himself, this can only be when we shall see Him *face to face, as He is (1 John 3:2), when "God [will] be all in all*. However, this cannot occur until we are released from our mortal bodies, which, according to the expression of the Apostle Paul, make us *absent from the Lord*. In other words, there is reason to believe, as people usually do, that every son of the Kingdom must expect the coming of the Kingdom of Heaven no earlier than the death of his own mortal body. According to this point of view, the coming of the Kingdom for all cannot be before *the Earth...will be burned up*.

> *1 Corinthians 13:12*
> *1 Corinthians 15:28*
> *2 Corinthians 5:6*
> *2 Peter 3:10*

However, before the coming of the eternal Kingdom of God, which must reveal itself in man after the temporal life and passing away of the world, the Lord indicates that there is a lesser form of His Kingdom, not quite attainable, not quite revealed, and partly existing in the present and party in the future. Some must seek and await this Kingdom, while for others, it is truly attainable: *There are some standing here who shall not taste death till they see the Son of Man coming in His Kingdom*. Who stood near the Lord when He spoke this mystical prophecy? We must examine their lives to see how this prophetic word was realized in their own lives, and what it actually meant.

> *Matthew 16:28*

From the Gospel account, we see that Jesus was with His Twelve Apostles, and that He spoke of His imminent coming to *His disciples*. According to another Evangelist, He spoke with them of the vision of the Kingdom of God *present with power*. How could the Apostles see it before they tasted death, and which of them were allowed to see it?

> *Matthew 16:24*
> *Mark 9:1*

Jesus Christ appeared in the world, *taking the form of a bondservant*, hiding the power of His Kingdom, or revealing only inklings of it in His mighty words and miracles. This was certainly the case before His death on the Cross. But after His Resurrection, He triumphantly announced to His disciples, *All authority has been given to Me in Heaven and on Earth*. Consequently, from the

> *Philippians 2:7*
> *Matthew 28:18*

moment of His Resurrection, they began to see the Son of man coming in His Kingdom.

The manifestations of the coming Kingdom were as follows. He ascended into the heavens, and sat at the right hand of God the Father. He once again appeared on Earth by sending the Holy Spirit down on the Apostles and other faithful. Through the mediation of the Spirit, He actively began to build a single well-established Church of His followers. Soon, the Kingdom of the Church spread from Judea to all the countries of the world with such speed that even during the life of the Apostles, it stretched from India to Spain, from Scythia to Ethiopia. The power of the apostolic preaching was so great that the blood of the martyrs defeated the persecutions of the Caesars. Then, without erring, the Apostles could truly agree with the Lord's prophecy that "there are some standing here who shall not taste death till they see the Son of Man coming in His Kingdom."

However, it is not difficult to note that the vision of the Son of Man coming into His Kingdom in power did not belong to all the Apostles. Judas the traitor was bereft of it, and so the Lord did not promise the vision to all: "there are some standing here..." And so, one cannot help but ask the question: who are the "some" who stand here?

To give a simple, yet accurate, answer to this question, we won't pontificate too long here, but instead we will simply read the Gospel: *'Assuredly, I say to you, there are some standing here who shall not taste death till they see the Son of Man coming in His Kingdom.' Now after six days Jesus took Peter, James, and John his brother, led them up on a high mountain by themselves; and He was transfigured before them. His face shone like the sun, and His clothes became as white as the light.* Why did the Evangelist indicate such an exact passage of time between His prophecy of the imminent Kingdom and the miracle of the Transfiguration? The only reason could be that he intended to connect the two events clearly. In other words, it's

Matthew 16:28-17:2

obvious that he intended us to understand that the Transfiguration was the fulfillment of the prophecy of the Kingdom.

And so, some of those standing near Jesus—that is, Peter, James, and John—saw Him coming in His Kingdom. They saw the Kingdom of God come in power when they saw His glorious Transfiguration. The divinity of Jesus shone through His humanity. Moses, the giver of the Law, stood before the Lord of the Law like a slave. Elijah, the zealot of the one true God came to worship the God-man. The voice of God the Father announced Jesus as His beloved Son and called all to worship Him as a king: *Hear Him!*. The blessed power of the heavenly Kingdom pierced through the Apostles, giving them ecstatic joy, and the life of Heaven almost swallowed up their physical life, so that the return from heavenly vision to earthly sensations seemed to them a kind of awakening from sleep, or, perhaps, it would be better to say that they fell asleep again into the half-dreaming state of earthly life.

Matthew 17:5

Some people might think that, yes, this is a wonderful vision, but what does it have to do with us, when the Lord promised such a vision only to a few chosen ones, and now that event itself has passed us by? But I think that everything in the entire earthly life of our Lord Jesus Christ touches us in some way directly. After all, was it not for our sake that He was born on Earth, lived, died, and rose again? Was it not for our salvation that he acted and spoke? It is absolutely true that He did everything necessary for our salvation. However, it is equally true that He did nothing excessive. It was necessary that after His appearance as a bondservant, but before His glorious Second Coming, He should initially and mysteriously reveal Himself coming in His Kingdom. It was necessary for His disciples, before tasting death, to see the Kingdom of God in power, at least for the blinking of an eye. This was demanded by the universal law of gradual revelation that is evident in all the actions and manifestations of God. This temporal revelation of the Kingdom of Heaven was necessary to prepare us for the difficult and dilatory revelation of its fullness to come.

Finally, this is an indication for us as well, that even in our current life, *we all, with unveiled face, beholding as in a mirror the glory of the Lord, are being transformed into the same image from glory to glory.* It is necessary for us also, after first laboring in repentance and the doing of the commandments like the slaves we are, to become sons of God through faith, prayer, and love, becoming transformed internally from earthly beings into heavenly ones. For only then, finally, can we be resurrected and raised up into the glorious life in the Kingdom of Heaven. If you do not have the Kingdom of God, come in power, within you before you die, then even after death you will not enter the Kingdom of God that abides in power. Amen.

2 Corinthians 3:18

10

Homily on the Transfiguration (1845)

Come, all who love the truth, for now your love is rewarded and satisfied by the perfect teachings of the most exalted Truth Himself. Come, you who are inattentive, or unhappy with the shortcomings and unworthiness of your teachers. Be attentive, for now you will hear the Teacher, whose virtues are limitless, and whose teaching is most excellent. From Tabor we hear the sermon not merely of a teacher of the Church, not even of an Apostle, Prophet, or even an Angel, but of God the Father Himself: *Behold a voice out of the cloud, which said, 'This is my beloved Son, in whom I am well pleased; hear Him'!*

<small>Matthew 3:17</small>

The teachers of the Church speak of two forms of salvific teaching: dogma and the commandments. Dogma is truth revealed by God that we must believe for our salvation. A commandment is a rule given by God that we must accomplish if we want to be saved.

Both forms of teaching are evident in the heavenly sermon. *This is my beloved Son, in whom I am well pleased.* This the dogma. "Hear him!" This is the commandment. Even earlier, at the Jordan River, we have already heard a divine dogmatic sermon. A

<small>Matthew 3:17</small>

voice came from Heaven saying: *This is my beloved Son, in whom I am well pleased*. That was a sermon directed at the first preacher of the New Testament, John the Baptist, and he was hardly alone in being able to understand it. *Matthew 3:17*

And so, he began to preach that which he heard from the heavens when he spoke of Christ: *He that comes from above is above all*, and *The Father loves the Son, and has given all things into his hand*. But John's preaching, along with his freedom and life, came to a quick end. Because of this, it was necessary for the dogma of the divinity of the Son of God to be preached again on Tabor for the sake of the three Apostles, for the affirmation of their faith, and to prevent our own lack of faith. According to the Law, the witness of three people was considered binding. *John 3:31, 3:35*

At that time, they were commanded to *tell the vision to no man, until the Son of Man be risen again from the dead*. However, as soon as this prohibition ended, the vision became one of the steadfast proofs of their witness to the divinity, power, and glory of Jesus Christ. *Matthew 17:9*

> *For we have not followed cunningly devised fables, when we made known unto you the power and coming of our Lord Jesus Christ, but were eyewitnesses of his majesty. For he received from God the Father honor and glory, when there came such a voice to him from the excellent glory, 'This is my beloved Son, in whom I am well pleased.' And this voice which came from Heaven we heard, when we were with him on the holy mount.*

2 Peter 1:16-18

Brethren, let us contemplate with awe and joy such holiness and such firmness of faith in Jesus Christ, the Son of God. Let us be unceasingly grateful to God, who revealed and affirmed it. *For God so loved the world that he gave his Only-begotten Son, that whosoever believes in him should not perish, but have everlasting life.* To prepare the world for His reception, *at sundry times and in divers manners [He] spoke in time past unto the fathers by the Prophets*, He foretold

John 3:16

Hebrews 1:1

and foreshadowed His coming through the Prophets and *the Law, having a shadow of good things to come.* [Hebrews 10:1]

When He came into the world, assuming our human nature, His miracles revealed His divine power, manifesting what was hidden beneath the veil. However, miracles demonstrating the presence of divine power do not decisively prove that the miracle worker is God Himself. Given that miracles can be done by men with the power of God, what else can be done to reveal Jesus to be the true Son of God? Should He announce Himself? He did so when He said, *I and my Father are One.* [John 10:30] His word was in and of itself the Truth, supported by His miracles. However, He recognized that self-witness is not enough for some: *If I bear witness of myself, my witness is not true.* [John 5:31]

Do you see how completely He overcomes this objection? God the Father, who *alone has immortality, dwelling in the light which no man can approach; whom no man has seen, nor can see,* [1 Timothy 6:16] came down from His invisible heights, bowed down the heavens, clothed His unapproachable light in a bright cloud visible to mortals, contained His limitless authority and revelation within a human voice, and preached Christ's divinity as united with the human form of Christ by calling Him His *beloved Son.* For the *beloved* Son is an *Only-begotten* Son, and an Only-begotten Son can be nothing but consubstantial with His Father.

Let us turn from dogma to commandment.

During Theophany, at the Jordan River, the dogma of the consubstantiality of the Father with the Son was proclaimed. The vision on Tabor added a commandment to this dogma, "Hear him!" In other words, you must listen to the teachings of the incarnate Son of God, as well as enter into an active obedience to Him, always abiding in this obedience.

It was unnecessary to utter a commandment of obedience to John at the Jordan, and it was too early to do so for all others. It was unnecessary for John, because he had already fulfilled this commandment when he baptized Jesus, for he overcame his own desire to be baptized by Jesus. For the others, it was too early. At the Jordan, Christ only revealed His face, not His teachings. And so, faith and vigilance were ignited, but not obedience to the teachings yet to be revealed.

On Tabor, the commandment of obedience was proclaimed according to the needs of the specific witnesses of the vision. For even Peter, who was greatest in faith and first among the Apostles to confess Jesus to be *the Christ, the Son of the living God*, was not prepared to ignore his own convictions through obedience to Christ's word: *From that time forth Jesus began to show his disciples how he must go unto Jerusalem, and suffer many things of the elders and chief priests and scribes, and be killed, and be raised again the third day. Then Peter took him, and began to rebuke him, saying, 'Be it far from You, Lord: this shall not done unto You'.* *Matthew 16:16*

Matthew 16:21-22

Though this rejection of the mystery of faith was quickly rebuked by the Lord, it seems that Peter's internal disposition required further healing. This healing was provided by Moses and Elijah while speaking to Jesus on Tabor, for they *spoke of His death which He should accomplish at Jerusalem*. They spoke of His imminent suffering and death on the cross. For them, this was a discussion of contemplation and prayer, while for Peter it was a continuation of that teaching about the cross that he feared to confront. It is most likely that this healing was completed by the heavenly Physician Himself. *Hear him!* In other words, though you may find it difficult to understand, though it speaks to you of suffering and the cross, though you have aspirations to earthly power and glory, you must submit to the teachings of the incarnate Son of God. *Luke 9:31*

It is also true that the dogma and commandment preached on Tabor were not meant for the three Apostles alone, but for all of us. Divine Truth does not speak to the Earth from the heavens for three people alone, but for the salvation of all mankind. *The voice of the Lord is powerful; the voice of the Lord is full of majesty.* He is *Psalm 29:4* not limited by place or time. Such was the power and authority thundering on Tabor for the three Apostles, and equally powerful is His voice in the Gospels for all of Christ's disciples. He commands with overwhelming authority, and He gives us the ability to accomplish the command through His unlimited power.

Brethren, consider that God the Father leads us to obedience to His beloved Son Jesus Christ through this same power and authority. Will anyone dare not submit to this divine authority? Who does not desire to accept the gift of obedience from this salvific power? *Hear him.* How can we fail to obey always and in all things? Will someone truly fail to hear Him?

John 14:1   The incarnate Son of God says, *believe in God, believe also in me.* Hear Him and make this faith the driving force of your lives!

Matthew 4:17   *Jesus began* and has not stopped *to preach, and to say, 'Repent: for the Kingdom of Heaven is at hand.'* Hear Him and hasten to reach His ever-nearing heavenly Kingdom through repentance. For justice is also near, yet He has not yet closed the doors of mercy.

Mount Tabor is not very tall, easily accessible to all. It is from such a height that the Lord Jesus teaches the nations. For his many different disciples, He shows various steps to blessedness. However, all these steps become a single path to salvation: "Blessed are the poor in spirit; Blessed are they that mourn; Blessed are the meek; Blessed are they which do hunger and thirst after righteousness; Blessed are the merciful, the pure in heart, the peacemakers"; and finally, *Blessed are they which are persecuted for*

Matthew 5:3-11   *righteousness' sake and for my sake.*

Hear the divine Teacher! If it seems difficult to climb the many steps to blessedness, then at least take the first step. Just take a step and continue to walk upward without laziness. Since you feel the sin within you, hold on to the step of repentance. It is perhaps rough and difficult to climb at first, but if you persist, it will become pleasant and will lead to the next step of unceasing hunger for righteousness. Not the righteousness of man, but the righteousness of God, given by Jesus Christ, *who of God is made unto us wisdom, and righteousness, and sanctification, and redemption.*   *1 Corinthians 1:30*

Whoever thinks highly of himself should hurry to the step of spiritual poverty, to the knowledge of his own nothingness. Whoever has a tendency to quarrel or disagree with others should hurry to the steps of meekness and inner peace, though it be with great effort. Exercise purity of heart, no less than purity of external works, for God's all-pure eye looks at the heart. Do not abandon the way of the cross, but listen to the words of the Lord, *If any man will come after me, let him deny himself, and take up his cross, and follow me.*   *Matthew 16:24*

Do not object to the message of the cross, like Peter. Do we not find great pleasure in enduring difficulties for someone we honor and love? Therefore, if we carry the cross of Christ willingly, we will find joy in the very act, even before we experience the promised blessedness. Let us not reject our cross! May we be crucified to our flesh, killing its lusts; may we be crucified to the world, not being enticed by its glimmer and glory; may we be crucified to our self-love, struggling to always act, speak, think, and live for Christ. May Christ live within us!

Christians! Obey Christ the Lord with everlasting obedience. For He *became the author of eternal salvation unto all them that obey him.* Glory to Him with the Father and Holy Spirit for all ages! Amen.   *Hebrews 5:9*

11

Homily on Palm Sunday (1825)

And this was done that it might be fulfilled which was spoken by the Prophet, saying: 'Tell the daughter of Zion, Behold, your King is coming to you, Lowly, and sitting on a donkey, a colt, the foal of a donkey' (Matthew 21:4-5).

How pleasant it is to see the reflection of the sun on pure water. Even though it shines not as powerfully as in the heavens, but its light shines in a way more accessible for the viewer. Similarly, it is also pleasant to contemplate with the spiritual eye (or with a mind directed toward God) the Sun of righteousness, our Lord Jesus Christ, in the pure waters of Israel, that is, in the prophetic words that flowed from the Spirit of God. Here, He is not presented with as much light as in the Gospels, but still in such a way that the attentive reader can easily see His divine qualities, His miraculous acts, and His profound and salvific mysteries.

Even the Evangelist Matthew considered it not excessive to show the glory and mystery of this present day through the expressions of the Prophet Zechariah. Let us read the exact words of the Prophet, which Matthew shortens somewhat in his gospel: *Rejoice greatly, O daughter of Zion! Shout, O daughter of Jerusalem! Behold, your King is coming to you; He is just and brings salvation, lowly and riding on a donkey, a colt, the foal of a donkey.* We can point out two interesting moments here: the miraculous event that was prophesied, and the proclamation of a new prophecy through the event itself.   *Zechariah 9:9*

Even if the event prophesied by Zechariah had not yet occurred, we would still be able to tell, by the prophecy itself, that the promised event would be miraculous. Who could ever imagine that any king would enter his own city in triumphant procession while riding a young foal of a donkey, a beast of burden? And if anyone did appear in this form, calling himself king, could anyone imagine that everyone would accept him with sincere joy and triumphant cries, instead of laughter and scorn? From ancient times, kings led triumphant processions while mounted on war horses; noblemen during peacetime, because of the simplicity of ancient customs, did travel on donkeys; however, any foal born of a donkey meant as a beast of burden, especially a young, untrained foal that still hadn't been separated from its mother-- would a king ever sit on such an animal?

What was it that inspired Zechariah to foretell the triumphant coming and meeting of the King, *lowly and riding on a donkey, a colt, the foal of a donkey*? How could such a prophecy ever be fulfilled? Both the fact that he had such a prophecy, and the possibility of its fulfillment, were nothing other than extraordinary, since they were prepared by God. Even the Jews admitted, from ancient times until now, that the unusual nature of Zechariah's prophecy concerning the meek king must refer to the Messiah, or to Christ Himself, though, alas! They! They do not recognize him in the meek Jesus.   *Zechariah 9:9*

But if we can see unusual events even in the prophecy of Zechariah alone, then let us all the more examine the actual event, to reveal even more of the miraculous and the openly divine.

When any king must enter the king's city triumphantly, the triumphant nature of his entry is made obvious by various preliminary plans and preparations. But we see nothing of the kind in the Lord's entry, not until the very day, almost until the very hour, of his kingly entry into Jerusalem. Yesterday He spent the night in Bethany, where He had resurrected Lazarus; and as His feet were anointed with oil, he spoke not of any preparations for His enthronement, but for His burial. There was a rather large crowd there, but *they came not for Jesus' sake only, but that they might also see Lazarus.* Today, in the morning, He goes to Jerusalem, accompanied by His disciples, just as on any other day. As St. Luke wrote, *When He had said this, He went on ahead, going up to Jerusalem.* There are no preparations. No one is even thinking of His enthronement as king. *His disciples did not understand these things at first.*

John 12:9

Luke 19:28

John 12:16

This event occurs suddenly and unexpectedly. *And it came to pass.* Before reaching Bethphage, not far from Jerusalem itself, He gives an unexpected command: *When He drew near to Bethphage and Bethany, at the mountain called Olivet, then He sent two of His disciples, saying, 'Go into the village opposite you, where, as you enter, you will find a colt tied, on which no one has ever sat. Loose it and bring it here.* Matthew adds: *a donkey tied, and a colt with her.*

Luke 19:29-30; Matthew 21:2

Note attentively how truly divinely does our divine King act. He sees the prophecy. He sees the imminent moment when it must be fulfilled; but as yet, He has no way of bringing it about. He looks not with His physical eyes, but with His omniscience, and the thing that is needed immediately reveals itself. *They found it just as He had said to them.* How miraculous that the Lord was able to find a way to accomplish the miracle, but no less miraculous is the manner in which the colt is taken.

Luke 10:32

Loose them and bring them to me, he said to two disciples. They could have easily answered: "Lord! How can we do such a thing? How can we take someone else's animal and take it to a place that the owner knows nothing about?" Truly, this could have

Matthew 21:2

disturbed the Apostles; truly, the apparent impossibility of the command could have been accompanied by the disobedience of those who were sent, since in other cases the troubles they encountered in the fulfillment of Jesus' commands were accompanied by their flight or even rejection of the Lord. Then, the entire event would have collapsed, and the prophecy would not have come to pass. But here the divine knowledge of our King foresaw the readiness of those He sent, and His divine power over their hearts strengthened them against any doubt. The same foreknowledge also anticipated the question of the owner of the colt: "Why are you loosing the colt?" That same authority over the hearts of men gave the seemingly feeble answer, not at all convincing under most circumstances, but said with incontestable conviction: *The Lord has need of him.* Luke 19:34

And so, those who were sent took the donkey, though they did not know to whom it belonged. And the owner gave it willingly to a man he didn't know, for no discernable reason. In the meantime, the large crowd, which was not called by the king, but which *had come to the feast*, came to meet Jesus, not because they were called by the voice of the herald, but because of the news of Lazarus's resurrection. Filled with sudden ecstasy, instead of prepared decorations they laid their own clothes at his feet. Instead of kingly banners and weapons, they took the branches of a tree. They walked before Him, they followed Him, they cried aloud to the meek King who was being calmly borne by a foal without any kingly pomp—a foal that had never before been trained by any human hand for any kind of burden. How did all these unexpected occurrences all happen at the same time? Truly, everything occurred so that *it might be fulfilled which was spoken by the prophet.* Matthew 21:4 That which was unfeasible did occur, so that it could be clearly seen that He for whom *nothing will be impossible* was now acting. Luke 1:37

John 12:12

We see the miraculous fulfillment of the prophecy of Zechariah. Let us focus our attention and see in the event itself a new prophecy of an even more wondrous event to come.

In actual fact, what is the significance of the kingly entrance of the Lord into Jerusalem? Why was such a wondrous prophecy necessary? Why so many miracles? What was the point of so many unexpected events? What is the consequence of these divine actions? What is the result of such a majestic, and yet such a quickly passing appearance, of the King of Zion? Like lightning, the heavenly Kingdom opens over Jerusalem, and like lightning, it is swallowed by the region of darkness. The people had only just begun to gather to meet the righteous King who would save them, and already unrighteousness is thinking of how to destroy both Him and Lazarus, who glorified Him: *But the chief priests plotted to put Lazarus to death also*. The children in the Temple were only just beginning to exclaim from the fullness of their pure hearts, and the leaders and wise men, *the chief priests and scribes… were indignant*, and from the overflowing of their hatred, they could not hide their indignation.

John 12:10

Matthew 21:15

Today the daughters of Zion proclaim: *Behold, your king is coming to you!*, but in a few days the same daughters of Zion, that is, the nation of Israel, will say, *We have no king*, and that very King will reject the visible semblance of kingship, saying, *My Kingdom is not of this world*. Today, they say, *Hosanna to the Son of David*, but soon they will say, *Crucify Him!* What is the purpose of this splendid, but passing, spectacle?

Matthew 21:5
John 19:15

John 18:36;
Matthew 21:9;
John 19:15

And here you might protest, "Did you not already say that all this occurred by the Prophet's word?" I said that this was so wondrously foretold for this reason: so that the prophecy could be recognized as the word of God, and it was accomplished so wondrously so that we could see this event as the action of God. But why did the word of God foretell this, and what followed God's action? When God, who *spoke, and they came to be*, and *indeed it was very good*, proclaims His word, His own action cannot fail to follow later. It is necessary that something essentially and firmly good occur as a result, not only a momentary mirage. And so, what is God doing here? Why is the word of God proclaimed, and

Psalms 32:9
Genesis 1:31

why does it include even seemingly insignificant details such as the age of the colt?

However, is it possible that such subtle questions in and of themselves are seemingly too brazen, without actually uncovering any truth? At the very least, do you not notice that in the glory of today's day, there must be some kind of mystery hidden, even if we have not yet come to reveal it? Do you not already have some idea, even if you cannot quite discern it? Having come to this point, lest I lose all credence before you, I will fall silent. Instead, let the holy Chrysostom answer this riddle and reveal this mystery to you:

> For here the church is signified by the colt, and the new people, which was once unclean, but which, after Jesus sat on them, became clean. And see the image preserved throughout. I mean that the disciples loose the asses. For by the Apostles, both they and we were called; by the Apostles were we brought near. But because our acceptance provoked them also to emulation, therefore the ass appears following the colt. For after Christ has sat on the Gentiles, then shall they also come moving us to emulation. And Paul declaring this, said, That blindness in part is happened to Israel, until the fullness of the Gentiles be come in; and so all Israel shall be saved. For that it was a prophecy is evident from what is said. For neither would the Prophet have cared to express with such great exactness the age of the ass, unless this had been so. But not these things only are signified by what is said, but also that the Apostles should bring them with ease. For as here, no man gainsaid them so as to keep the asses, so neither with regard to the Gentiles was any one able to prevent them, of those who were before masters of them.
>
> But He does not sit on the bare colt, but on the Apostles' garments. For after they had taken the colt, they then gave

Romans 11:25-26

up all, even as Paul also said, *I will very gladly spend and be spent for your souls.*

But mark how tractable the colt, how being unbroken, and having never known the rein, he was not restive, but went on orderly; which thing itself was a prophecy of the future, signifying the submissiveness of the Gentiles, and their sudden conversion to good order. For all things did that word work, which said, loose him, and bring him to me: so that the unmanageable became orderly, and the unclean thenceforth clean.

So much for the holy Chrysostom. Let us repeat the teaching of this mystery of Christ to perhaps make it even more understandable. The entry of the Lord into Jerusalem is not simply an expression of the present, but is even more a prophecy and a sign of His future enthronement as King. His Kingdom is not this Jerusalem, which will be soon destroyed, nor is it the land of Judea, which will soon be enslaved and emptied, but the Church, against which *the gates of Hades shall not prevail.* The donkey and the colt on which He sits for His kingly triumph symbolize the two races of people over whom He will spiritually rule — the Jews and the Gentiles. The beast of burden is a symbol of the Jews, who have long borne the burden of the Law on their shoulders, a yoke as the best of them even admitted: *which neither our fathers nor we were able to bear,* a yoke that they had to shed for the sake of the easy yoke and light burden of Christ.

The untrained colt is a symbol of the pagans who have not yet been tamed by the teaching, who have not yet learned the Law. The Apostles take both the donkey and the colt without any hindrance. That is, the Apostles, in spite of external obstacles, will submit both the Jews and the Gentiles to the Kingdom of Christ. The Lord sits on the colt; the donkey follows. In other words, at first, for the most part it will be the Gentiles who will submit to the Kingdom of Christ, and when the foreordained from among the pagans enter into the fullness of the Church, then the remaining Jews will turn back and overtake them.

The untrained colt calmly bears the King; that is, the unlearned and self-willed Gentiles will soon become orderly by the teaching and commandments of Christ. They lay down clothes before the King. That means that the complete followers of Christ give Him everything of theirs. The children accept and glorify the King; that is, the hearts of mankind, child-like in their simplicity and sincerity, accept Christ through faith and glorify Him through love.

O Christians! Sons of the Kingdom of Christ! If we see the glory, or if we pierce through to the mystery of today's feast, let us not allow it to pass by us as a spectacle that has nothing to do with us, for in this case we will remain outside of the Kingdom of Christ. Is the Lord calling any one of us to special service? Let us be obedient without retorting, like the Apostles. Does He require anything of us? Let us give Him everything without complaint, just as the owner of the donkey gave up his property. Let us do it willingly, even if it results in a loss of something necessary for us, as did those who laid their own clothing at his feet.

Has any one of you walked in the self-will of his own heart up until this moment? Now is the time to bow down under the yoke of Christ. Does anyone think that he can become virtuous by following a moral law? Follow Christ, *if you want to be perfect*. Matthew 19:21 Let us all cry out with our child-like, sincere hearts, *Hosanna to the Son of David!* Matthew 21:9

We will *have this man to reign over us* for all ages. Amen. Luke 19:14

12

A Homily on Pascha (1811)

Christ is risen!

Psalm 85:12   He has risen, O Christians! *Truth shall spring out of the earth*, from the tomb where the lies of men and the justice of God had consigned Him. The seal that faithlessness placed upon the Truth's cold tomb melted away because of the flame of divinity that lay within it. The heavy stone of temptation covering it fell, destroying the disobedience of the Jews and the arrogance of the Greeks. This tomb, within which *Romans 8:19*   lay the *expectation of all creatures*, is now empty, and an Angel sits at the head of the tomb and writes on it. He does not merely write on the ugly headstone of a dead man, but rather he writes an epigraph that from this moment forward will be true of all who die. He writes *O death, where is your sting? O grave, where is your 1 Corinthians 15:55*   *victory?*

How amazing that one moment can change the fate of the world! I do not recognize Hell; I cannot distinguish between Heaven and Earth. Is Hell the place that held slaves captive but now releases the sons of freedom? Is Earth the place where divinity shines in heavenly glory? Is Heaven the place where the earthborn reside and humanity reigns? It is an ineffable change, to go from complete starvation to perfect fullness, from profound poverty to the most exalted bliss, from death to immortality, from Hell to Heaven, from man to God! O glorious Pascha! Rejoice in this Pascha, O joyful wanderers of a miserable land! *And this day shall be unto you for a memorial; and you shall keep it a feast to the Lord throughout your generations; you shall keep it a feast by an ordinance forever.* Exodus 12:14

Let us further examine the characteristics of the eternal Passover. By doing so, we will better understand the depth of its triumph.

Pascha means "Passover," a feast initially established among the Jews. Their Pascha signified the "passing over" of the avenging Angel, the destruction of the first-born of Egypt, the exodus from the house of slavery, and deliverance from a fierce tyrant. The lamb, eaten after being ritually prepared, was a symbol and remembrance of the event.

Though their lives were preserved in Egypt, they were quickly lost in a terrifying way in the desert. Though they joyfully left the house of slavery, they wept countless tears during the forty years of wandering. Did the deliverance of such a people, who later became a model of tragedy, warrant eternal celebration? However, the eternal Wisdom determined to show His disciples the eventual fate of this people. His Pascha fulfilled and replaced the one that came before.

This is how, *in these last days*, these things, which were mysteries to the ancients, were revealed. Jesus Christ, a Lamb in meekness, perfected mankind by uniting with mankind. Like the sacrificial lamb, He is male, for He has the strength to carry our infirmities. He is immaculate in His purity, for He is free even of ancestral sin. He is like a yearling lamb, meaning he has reached His adulthood; He is slain on the cross, tempered by the fire of Hebrews 1:2

God's justice, and gives himself as spiritual food to the spiritual *tribe of Abraham*[1].

At the Mystical Supper, He is eaten with the *unleavened bread of sincerity and truth*, consumed whole without leaving any remnant. Ancestral sin poisons all thoughts and desires in the sons of this age, making them only produce dead works. However, the sacramental Blood of Christ, when sprinkled on the souls of the faithful, revives the source of their heavenly lives. Through His Passover, He frees us from enslavement to sin; the bitter herbs, that is, sensual desires and vanity, no longer distract from constant service to God. Finally, the invisible Pharaoh, the *ruler of the darkness of this world*, is brought to total exhaustion.

1 Corinthians 5:8

Ephesians 6:12

This, dear listeners, is the new, blessed Pascha, a transfiguration of the old Passover.

However, the triumph is not yet complete and fulfilled. There is a mystery still hidden within the house of preparation, that is, within the soul. Though we approach God with our inner man, we remain in the world with our outer man. Partaking in the grace of faith cannot immediately destroy the curse that has wormed itself into our human nature. That is why we must add *bitter herbs* into our spiritual meal. We are often attacked by sorrows and temptations. We must partake of the mysterious food with *haste*, and save ourselves by fleeing this obstinate generation.

Exodus 12:8

Exodus 12:11

We must have our *loins girded with truth*, taking part in ceaseless exploits against our foes. The staff of boldness must be *in our hand*, for we are threatened at every step with stumbling and falling. We must have *shoes on our feet*, for the ancient serpent still bruises our heel, sharpening its dull fangs on our flesh, in spite of having been dealt a fatal blow to its head.

Ephesians 6:14

Exodus 12:11

Exodus 12:11

Genesis 3:15

Oh, poor flesh! O slothful dust that suffocates the industrious spirit! O burden that pursues me even as I flee the world!

---

1 Throughout this homily, St. Philaret references the Passover as related in Exodus 12:5-8. Not all the references are in italics.

O treacherous friend, O vile foe! Helper – traitor! Fearsome – beloved! Where will I hide from you? I make peace with you, having not defeated you. Not having time to enjoy the peace, I continue railing against you. You groan when I exhaust you, you wish for me to indulge you. Sharp thorns pierce you, but aromatic roses plunge you into sloth and relaxation. You serve as a target for the fiery arrows of the evil one and even cover up his intrigues.

I strive toward the light of Zion, but you hold me back within the darkness of Egypt. Sometimes you cry out to the Lord in anguish that you do not even understand. But as soon as you come near to the source of life, like Mary Magdalene, you still search for the dead body, for sensual pleasures. The Lord tells you *do not touch me*; and your own soul has no choice but to agree with the Lord's judgment. *John 20:17*

Who of us is safe from these temptations, which sometimes even crush those we believe to be vessels of grace? For while serving *the Lord with fear*, we can *rejoice* in Him only with *trembling*. *Psalm 2:11* We are allowed to *taste and see that the Lord is good* but we cannot yet fill ourselves with this meal. Even our own new Pascha, which had been prefigured in the Old Testament, is itself another prophecy of the final Pascha. *Psalm 34:8)*

The triumphant final Passover of Israel had to happen in the Promised Land, *at the place which the Lord your God shall choose*, in the presence of God in Jerusalem, *the city of your rest*. Similarly, the fulfillment of our Pascha will occur when we stop our lives of earthly wandering. As the Ark of the Covenant divided the waters of Jordan for Israel to walk through, so the tomb of our resurrected Mediator of the New Covenant will grant us safe passage through the waters of death that fill our life. *Deuteronomy 16:6* *Sirach 36:15*

We will throw away our old bodies, like the rags of exiles, and we will ascend to the Jerusalem on high. Then, it will not be the doors of the earthly temple, but God's own eternal tabernacle that will open before us. The ageless Lamb shall appear to us no longer in the mystery of communion, but in the undimmed brilliance of His righteousness. The meal is rich, we will never hunger or overindulge! The bread is angelic, the wine is new, leading not to life but immortality! No longer mere joy, but ecstasy. Then the eternal Pascha will unite with the eternal Passover, the eternal ascent to God with eternal rest in Him.

This, dear listeners, is how we must understand today's feast. Since the triumphant Pascha of eternity has not yet come, and the mystical Pascha of internal unity with Christ is hidden from us, the Church shows us a glimpse of the first, and in a certain way opens the way to the other, through the festivities of Bright Week. The more our celebration models the great mystery of Christian teaching and piety — that is, reconciliation and unification with God — the more complete it is, the greater it is.

However, what if some of us limit Pascha to seven days of partying, never giving time to even think of coming closer to Christ? What if we expect to be *satisfied with the fatness* of the house of God, but do not want to partake of a single drop of the bitter chalice of Jesus? What if, instead of holding vigil over ourselves, we indulge in pagan carelessness on the days of the Church's feasts? *The people sat down to eat and drink, and rose up to play.* What if we are stuck in our old man in the middle of the feast of spiritual freedom, the new Pascha? What if we rejoice in the Resurrection, but remain dead to God?

Psalm 36:8

1 Corinthians 10:7

What kind of feast will this be? This sort of feast will be a body without a soul. For these kinds of Christians—it is frightening yet necessary to say this—there is no Resurrection of Christ. For *we are buried with him by baptism into death: that just as Christ was raised up from the dead by the glory of the Father, even so we also should walk in newness of life.*

Romans 6:4

O great and sacred Pascha of Christ! Teach us to celebrate the temporal Pascha with righteousness and grace, making us worthy to celebrate the coming eternal Pascha in glory. Amen.

13

Homily on Holy Pascha (1822)

Christ is risen!

No matter how many times we may have already repeated this phrase, we are still not tired of it, and we hope that you will not tire to hear the same words over and over again, "Christ is risen!"

What wonderful words! How these words change the form of everything that exists!

Until the time of Christ's Resurrection, many people only knew the Earth on which they appeared for a short time, and from which they soon disappeared, they knew not where. Others had heard something about Hell as a kind of pit that threatens to swallow everyone and allows no one to escape. Not many thought of Heaven as an exalted home that has a ladder leading to it that someone saw in a dream—and there were no people on that ladder, only Angels going up and down.

Now, when "Christ is risen," what becomes of the Earth? It becomes a seed bed for Heaven. The bodily life of a person is short and ends with destruction. The bodily life of a human being is the preparatory life of a chick in an egg, for which, after the breaking of the egg, a higher and fuller kind of life opens up. All that is needed is for the chick to be surrounded, filled up, and given life by the warmth of the mother's blood. That is, it is necessary for the embryo of the heavenly life in man to be surrounded, filled up, and given life by the life-giving power of the blood of Christ.

Now, when Christ is risen, and when to Him, as to the God-man, *all authority has been given...in Heaven and on Earth*, not only has Heaven become attainable, but it has become united with the Earth in such a way that it is difficult to find the limit or difference between them. For God appears on Earth, and humanity appears in Heaven as well. The Angels, whom Jacob saw going up and down the ladder leading to Heaven, now walk in hosts on the Earth as the messengers of the Son of man, who is the Lord of heaven.

Matthew 28:18

What becomes of Hell now, when, after His descent into it, "Christ is risen"? The Victor has entered the stronghold as though He were a prisoner; the prison whose gates are broken and whose guards have been scattered--this is truly, in Christ's icon, the monster that swallowed the Prophet who had been thrown off the ship. But, instead of swallowing and destroying him, it became for him a different ship, though not so calm, and it still brought him to the shore of life and safety. Now it becomes clear how the Psalmist believed he could pass through Hell itself without being harmed: *Yea, though I walk through the valley of the shadow of death, I will fear no evil, for You are with me.* You, who came down from Heaven for us, walked on Earth like us, and like us descended into the shadow of death, so that from there You might lay the path for Your followers to the light of life.

Psalm 22:4

Finally, has not the Resurrection of Christ made us different than before? Let us believe a true testament to the Resurrection of Christ—that it gave us new birth, if not in actual fact, then at least in hope. *Blessed be the God and Father of our Lord Jesus Christ, who according to His abundant mercy has begotten us again to a living hope through the Resurrection of Jesus Christ from the dead.*   *1 Peter 1:3*

But, if we are given new birth by the Resurrection of Christ only in *a living hope*, and following our hope is the hope of all creation, *or the earnest expectation of the creation eagerly waits for the revealing of the sons of God*, then all miracles that were created by the Resurrection of Christ are nothing but the first fruits of miracles yet to come, which will be revealed in the continuation, especially in the end times, and even in endless eternity.   *Romans 8:19*

Because of these endless miracles that have occurred and must yet occur, the Resurrection of Christ is for us a source of rumination, contemplation, wonder, joy, gratitude, and hope. It is always new, no matter how long ago or how many times we have drawn from it; it is eternal newness itself. And for this reason, no matter how sure we may be that each of us knows of the Resurrection of Christ, we still desire to tell each other a thousand times, as though it were an unknown bit of news, that "Christ is risen!" No matter how sure we are of the historicity of this event, which was witnessed by the eye-witnesses of the Resurrected One, which was proven by many signs and miracles, which was not even doubted by the enemies of Christianity, we still yearn yet to hear the confirmation that "Truly He is risen!"

If the Word is food, as it was written, for *man shall not live by bread alone; but man lives by every word that proceeds from the mouth of the Lord*, then the Word concerning the Resurrection of Christ, like manna, as the Preacher expresses it, is *ready-made bread from Heaven, fitting for every pleasure and suitable to every taste*. Are you exhausted by sin, and do you hunger for righteousness? Come, be fed! Christ is risen, *Who was delivered for our offenses, and was raised again for our justification*. Are you tired by the joyless burden of the Law, and do you desire to pass from this slavery into grace-filled freedom? Come, taste the Passover that you desire: *For even Christ our Passover is sacrificed for us. Stand fast therefore*   *Deuteronomy 8:3*

Wis. of Solomon 16:20

Romans 4:25

1 Corinthians 5:7

in the liberty wherewith Christ has made us free, and be not entangled again with the yoke of bondage. Galatians 5:1

Are you filled with the fear of death? Accept the proper medicine against this disease: *Christ is risen from the dead, and become the first fruits of them that slept.* Are you growing weak in your battle against the enemies of your salvation? *Taste the good word* of God's Resurrection, and in it the triumphant power of the age to come, *Let God arise, and let His enemies be scattered!* Are you deluded by the false taste of the sensual, and does it force you to seek your food in perishable and vain desires of the things of this world? Heal this disease with the communion of the power of the Resurrection: *If you are then risen with Christ, seek those things which are above, where Christ sits on the right hand of God.* Or has your soul *thirsted for the mighty living God* already, and are you filled with the desire to know *when shall I come and appear before God's face?* The living hope in the Resurrection will fill that hunger and yet preserve that hunger, for it is healthy and salvific, because it shows the mind that *when Christ, who is our life, shall appear, then shall you also appear with Him in glory.*

Do you see, O Christian, what an abundance, what variety of spiritual food our Passover, the resurrected Christ, offers us? Is your soul fed with it? Do you truly taste *that the Lord is good*? Do you feel inside yourself the power of the Resurrection of Christ, that frees you from sins, from the curse of having sinned, that hews down the passions and desires of the old man, that builds in you a pure heart and a renews a right spirit in your heart, that can support you in faith and hope, and that arouses in you a flame of love for the Giver of life?

Or are you still hungry and thirsty even at the table of the Lord? Or is your soul still not filled and empty? For all that, we do not desire through this question to lead you into confusion or despair! On the contrary. Even though godly sorrow is salvific, this is not a time for sorrow, but joy, which can also have its salvific effect: *for this day is holy unto our Lord; neither be sorry, for the joy of the Lord is your strength.* And so, have you tasted the goodness of the Resurrected One? May your soul rejoice in the Lord, and may this joy push you toward the closest union with Him.

Nehemiah 8:10
Psalm 34:9

Have you not yet tasted His goodness? And yet, all will rejoice, for He does not keep you from this taste, but calls you to it, giving you the possibility of hearing the good news of His Resurrection and of being among those who have gathered in the name of the Resurrected One, whereby His promise He is also among them. If you feel yourself to be unworthy of this joy, yet still be joyful for that wondrous goodness that does not reject even the unworthy from participation in this joy. May the joy of the Resurrection of our Lord implant in all of us the life-bearing and salvific power of His Resurrection. For the joy of the Lord is our power. Amen.

Matthew 28:20

14

A Homily on Pascha (1824)

Christ is risen!

Psalm 144:13   Truly, *The Lord is faithful in all His words.* As He went to His willful sufferings, He told His disciples, *I will see you again, and your heart shall rejoice, and your joy no man will take from you.* After His suffering, death, and Resurrection, when His work was finished on the Earth, His flesh itself no longer held Him down on the Earth, being freed from mortality. When His entire body felt the impulse to ascend to His heavenly Father, He said, *I ascend unto my Father.* And yet, He delayed on the Earth to give the promised joy to His earthly brothers.

John 16:22

John 20:17

He appeared to His disciples, who were gripped with fear and sadness, and He healed their heartsickness with the word, *Rejoice!* He appeared to His disciples, who had been *sifted as wheat* by Satan, and who had fled from the Jews, fell apart, and hid. He annihilated all danger with words of peace: *Jesus came and stood in the midst, and said to them, 'Peace be with you'.* Exactly as He had foretold, they saw Him, and their hearts rejoiced: *Then the disciples were glad when they saw the Lord.*

Matthew 28:9
Luke 22:31

John 20:19

John 20:20

If you want to be assured that their joy truly could not be taken away from them, observe how these people reacted after the Resurrection. Only recently, they had been defeated by their own faint-heartedness. Even the strongest of them had fallen down at the meaningless word of a slave, like a leaf blown away by wind. And what do we see? After these same people were convicted by the highest court of their land, receiving beatings and a strict prohibition to speak of Jesus, this is what happened: *They departed from the presence of the council, rejoicing that they were counted worthy to suffer shame for His name.* Acts 5:41

These events prove that the joy of the Resurrection of Christ cannot be taken away from those who receive it as a gift. After many centuries have passed, that joy is still as vibrant as it was on its first day, still as full and complete in the hearts of the truly faithful.

Blessed is he whose heart has acquired the joy of the resurrected Savior and who does not lose it! The gathering of the disciples of Christ, that is, the Church, has always had this joy. But every disciple, every individual member of the Church, may or may not have it, or he may find it sooner or later. Even the Apostle Thomas only acquired the full joy of the Resurrection of Christ eight days after the other Apostles. No force can take this joy away from those who carefully and fiercely guard it in their heart. But anyone can lose this divine joy by exchanging it for some worldly, insignificant joy, or he can lose it through negligence.

Christians! Judging by external appearances, I can assume that all of us, or at least most of us, have today acquired the joy of the Resurrection. This past holy night, this joy illumined the whole Church with a light as bright as the middle of the day. Each one of us received an oil lamp like the wise virgins who walked out to greet the heavenly Bridegroom. This joy has filled most of the liturgy with triumphant singing and exclamations.

This joy shone upon faces and clothes; it is written on our lips and signed with our kisses.

These are all powerful signs, but is all this the same joy promised by the Source of our joy? Does our joy have the conviction of the true joy that cannot be taken away from, the joy "no man will take from you"? The feast will continue, but perhaps it will only be celebrated in our idleness from our daily work. Or perhaps we may even turn to reprehensible actions, to sensual pleasures, to vain amusements. Let us instead abstain from our passions, let us instead replace the sensual impressions of our mind with the light of God, acquired through sacred reading and prayer. Let us guard our heart from any earthly desire, giving our hearts calm in the love of God, with the help of faith and hope.

The feast will pass; the time for work will come, we will wake up early for worldly work, for the needs and the profit of our mortal life. Then, perhaps, the joy of the Resurrection will not only start to fall asleep, but will die in our hearts and get buried in the dust and filth of earthly cares. Shouldn't we be honest that this could happen to us? If so, then we must admit that today's ordinary joy is nothing but a superficial, incomplete image, or rather a shadow of the true, inner, perfect joy that the Lord gives to His faithful servants or His chosen friends. Blessed is he, I will say again, who *enter[s] into the joy of [the] Lord*, whose soul does not remain in darkness when the festal candles burn out, who does not cease *singing and making melody in [the] heart to the Lord* when the triumphant singing in church falls silent.

Matthew 25:21

Ephesians 5:19

Perhaps someone is jealous of those who feel this immortal joy. Or perhaps some of you regret losing this much-desired joy. Whichever you are, you might ask. *Why isn't everyone given such joy?*

Ephesians 5:19

Here is my answer. The source of universal joy gives it to all without holding anything back. Since He died for all, and rose again for all, the fruit of His death and resurrection—immortal joy—belongs to all. But not everyone attains that which is given to everyone, not everyone can own that which belongs to all. Does it not seem strange that some of us cannot use this gift that is offered and given for free? However, there is doubt that this is what we actually see.

Thomas told the other Apostles who professed joy in the Resurrection: *I will not believe.* By doing so, He did not partake of the joy until the Lord—marvelous in truth and abundant in mercy—arrived especially for Thomas. While punishing Thomas's small lack of faith with a short deprivation of joy, He saw that in spite of it, Thomas had not left the disciples or deviated from His word. And so, out of love, Jesus came to him and allowed him to partake of the joy of the Resurrection by touching the life-giving wounds of His resurrected body with his own hands. *John 20:25*

Christ transformed temporary disbelief into an eternal witness to the truth. Though they had been previously defiled by the words of unbelief, now the lips of the Apostle are purified with a strong confession of faith: *My Lord and my God!* *John 20:28*

Thomas's experience gives rise to a new question: why did Jesus not use this same method of imparting conviction and joy in His Resurrection with many other people? In other words, why did He not allow others to have the same physical sensation, or obvious revelation, of His resurrected body? Especially since He Himself gives joy to others through the unmediated action of His presence, as He said, *I will see you again and your heart will rejoice.* What a daring question! Who can demand accountability from the Lord for His actions or be accountable in His stead? And where can we find an answer, so necessary to rebuke the brazenness of these inquirers, who are far more infected by faithlessness than Thomas? *John 16:22*

I hear this same question from the lips of the Apostles: *Lord, how is it that You will manifest Yourself to us, and not to the world?*. What can be better than hearing the answer to this question from the Lord Himself? But even He does not give a direct answer to this question. Nor did the Apostles ask this question *John 14:22* again after the Resurrection, when the world tried in every way possible to hide the glory of the Resurrection with its lies and slander.

How strange! A question is asked, but an answer is not given. However, it is clear that the question was answered, for the Apostles didn't ask a second time, even when the answer was much more necessary than before. How was it answered? We are left to guess that it was resolved for the Apostles by some other teaching of the Lord, or by direct enlightenment by the Holy Spirit, or through the experience of the miraculous actions and manifestations of the Lord.

Let us imagine, for the sake of argument, that the Lord appeared to the same gathering of priests that out of jealousy convicted Him to death. Do you think the proof of His Resurrection would have brought the Jews to faith and led to their salvation? Not in the least! The opposite has already been shown by experience.

Lazarus' Resurrection happened in front of all the people, and any person who wanted could see the resurrected Lazarus. But what reaction did this obvious miracle inspire in the members of the priestly class? They only became more hardened in their vicious lack of faith. *But the chief priests plotted to put Lazarus to death also.* And so, the Lord did not want to appear to them, and does not appear to those that are like them, because for those people who are hardened in unbelief, such appearances are useless; in fact, they only increase their lack of faith, to their greater condemnation.

John 12:10

Or let us suppose that they, being amazed by the sight of the resurrected Christ, would have been forced to call Him their Lord. What would have followed? Together with Peter, who was praised for his confession of Christ as the Son of God, you would also see Caiaphas, the initiator of the idea of deicide, as a confessor of Christ. Except he would not have come to the Kingdom of Heaven as a penitent sinner desiring salvation, but as a criminal caught in the act, someone who had nowhere else to go. Are these the kinds of sons of the Kingdom that the heavenly Kingdom awaits? Even earthly kingdoms would not accept them as members!

The Lord is wise in that He does not want to appear to the world in the glory of His Resurrection until the appointed time. He gives enough signs of Himself so that the willing can come to know and find Him. However, He does not dazzle everyone with miracles, lest he mix up the worthy sons of the Kingdom, who accepted him sincerely and freely, with unworthy slaves who only feign submission because they have been forced to. He warned the Apostles of this when He said: *The Kingdom of God does not come with observation.* *Luke 17:20*

Finally, we can also suppose, not without good reason, that the Lord spares the sons of the world by not appearing to them. For can dry grass withstand the presence of fire in the way that gold can? Would He not instantly burn the grass to ash and dust? The presence of the divine Jesus is similar. It strengthens the poor in faith, and it constantly purifies and illumines the faithful and righteous. If His presence were revealed to the faithless, to those rotting in sinfulness, would He not burn them? Would He not destroy them with His purity and power?

After all, what strikes down the greatest adversary of Christ, *the lawless one [whose coming] is according to the working of Satan, with all power, signs, and lying wonders?* What exalted power? What divine weapon? A single breath or word alone, the presence of the Lord Jesus alone: *The Lord will consume with the breath of His mouth and destroy with the brightness of His coming.* Inside Saul, the persecutor of Christianity, the chosen vessel of Christ, Paul, was already hidden. Even he was almost destroyed when the power of Christ's appearance suddenly touched him before he was prepared for it. He fell to the ground, blinded by Christ's light, trembling in terror. With his open eyes, he could see no one.

2 Thessalonians 2:9

2 Thessalonians 2:8

O son of dust, stop brazenly tempting and irritating the Lord of glory by competing with Him. Stop demanding that He appear for your edification or consolation. Instead, ask yourself: what makes you incapable of receiving His joy-giving manifestation? What can you do to prepare yourself for it, to make yourself worthy of it? This is a good question; therefore, and there is a clear and direct answer to it, given by the divine Teacher Himself: *If anyone loves Me, he will keep My word; and My Father will love him, and We will come to him and make Our home with him.*

<small>John 14:23</small>

Here is the law and the proper order of the blessed manifestations of the divine Savior! Just as a glass vessel must be cleaned, then warmed gradually to withstand heat, so the easily fractured structure of human nature must first be cleansed by studying the word of God, and by constantly exercising God's commandments, and by being warmed by love for God.

<small>Hebrews 12:29</small>
<small>John 1:9</small>
<small>2 Peter 1:19</small>
<small>2 Corinthians 3:18</small>

Then God, though He is *a consuming fire*, will not destroy him with His holy presence. Instead, the *light* of Christ *which gives light to every man coming into the world* will dawn on him, resurrecting him from the darkness of night, rising like *the morning star* in his heart. Then he will be able to *with unveiled face, behold ...the glory of the Lord* in Christ, and not only rejoice but also be *transformed into the same image from glory to glory...by the Spirit of the Lord.*

<small>John 20:2</small>
<small>John 20:6, 8</small>
<small>John 20:29</small>

This is exactly how the Lord appeared on the actual day of His Resurrection. The *disciple, whom Jesus loved* above all others, and who loved Him more than all others with a deep love of the spirit, received before all others, within the depths of his soul, the visitation and joy of the Resurrected One, when he saw *the linen cloths lying* in the tomb of the Lord. At that moment, he believed in the Resurrection: *and he saw and believed.* Because of this, it seems to me that the Lord was speaking of John, in a mysterious, grace-filled way, when He told Thomas: *Blessed are those who have not seen and yet have believed.*

<small>Mark 16:9</small>
<small>Luke 7:47</small>

Mary Magdalene, out of whom the Lord *cast out seven demons*, forgiving *her sins, which [were] many...for she loved much*, loved Him with a vivid and fiery love of the heart. And so, it was she who first saw His visible manifestation. "He rose early on the first day of the week, He appeared first to Mary Magdalene, out of whom He had cast seven demons" (Mark 16:9).

Christian! Do you believe in the words of the Lord: "I am with you always, *even* to the end of the age" (Matt. 28:20)? If you believe, then you must believe also that even in our present days, as in the first days of the Resurrection, the Lord appears to those who believe in Him and love Him. His manifestations are more or less obvious, depending on the level of their readiness and ability. He comes to them and gives His divine joy and peace to their hearts. Continue, then, to ascetically labor, even in these holy days, so that you may attract a grace-filled visitation through fervent prayer, through careful study of the word of God, through your good deeds according to the commandments of the Lord, and through your fiery love for the One who died and rose again for you.

Call the heavenly Guest to yourself more persistently, prepare yourself for His visitation more assiduously than you do for your earthly guests. And if He visits you with His divine consolation, be careful that "your joy no one will take from you" (John 16:22). Do not weigh down your heart with the pleasures of the world and the flesh. Just as a lantern dropped into water or mud goes out, so also your spiritual joy will go out if you plunge your heart into the pleasures of the flesh or the passions of the world. Then, your soul, as it is cast out from the bridal chamber, will once again be overwhelmed by darkness and death. May the Lord Jesus Christ—our light, life, and joy for all ages—protect us from such a fate. Amen.

15

Homily on Holy Pascha (1825)

Christ is risen!

"And He opened their understanding, that they might comprehend the Scriptures" (Luke 24:45).

How many churches are open! How many doors are unlocked today by a single key of David, by a single movement of that key!

At home, we bolt and lock our doors to prevent a thief from entering, or to prevent an unruly child from leaving. The same is true of the house of God. When the gardener and protector of the Paradise of God stole the fruit from the tree of knowledge, then was he cast out, Paradise was locked, and a protector stronger than he, with a fiery sword, was placed at the door. And since the transgressor needed to be punished still more, and since even after his exile his descendants continued to be governed by a spirit of transgression and rebellion, then both he and his descendants, one after the other, were led through the door of death to a prison where they were held not for days, but for the ages. From this, it is clear that the house of the Lord—that is, the Heaven that was meant to be entered through the garden of Eden—was locked and closed against this unworthy child of the house.

Finally, the only-begotten Son of the Father of the heavenly habitations, according to His mercy and His love for mankind, came to free the prisoners and to return the exiles. The Key of David, who opens all doors, is the God-manhood of Christ, who through His divinity imbues all human states, and through His humanity enters the hidden sanctum of the divinity. The all-opening action of this key is the Resurrection of Christ. With it, the prison is opened and the prisoners freed; Eden is opened, and the exiles are welcomed back; Heaven is opened, and it awaits the chosen. That which I have now said is also spoken by the Church visually by offering to you all, throughout the whole of today's feast, the opened doors to the altar table of the divine mysteries.

Let us also note another door that this same key of David opens. It might not be very large, but it does lead to a great treasure-house of God. "And he opened their understanding," writes the holy Evangelist. Then the Lord opened the minds of the Apostles. When was this? Then, when He resurrected, He appeared to them, showing them His wounds; He ate with them, and then He completely confirmed their faith in His Resurrection. "He opened their understanding, that they might comprehend the Scriptures. Then He said to them, *Thus it is written, and thus it was necessary for the Christ to suffer and to rise from the dead on the third day, and that repentance and remission of sins should be preached in His name to all nations, beginning at Jerusalem.* Let the mind of everyone listening to these words be opened as well, so that he may accept this important truth: the Resurrection of Christ, and faith in this Resurrection, opens the shut-up mind of man to the true knowledge of exalted and salvific objects of study. *Luke 24:45-47*

In actual fact, it had been a long time since *Jesus began to preach and to say, 'Repent, for the Kingdom of Heaven is at hand'*. And before *Matthew 4:17* all others, the Apostles were the first to listen to this preaching. It had been a very long time since they were sent out with the same preaching word: *The Kingdom of Heaven is at hand*. Thus, it was for a long time that they heard preaching concerning repentance and the Kingdom of God, and they themselves also preached about it; and yet, were their minds truly closed off to this truth? It's almost incredible, and yet, according to the word of the Lord, it is true. It was only after His Resurrection that He opened their understanding of the Holy Scriptures, and then, He spoke to them as those who already knew it: "thus it was necessary... that repentance and remission of sins should be preached." Until this moment, they saw repentance as a labor; now, however, they knew it more profoundly as repentance in the name of Jesus, as the soul and power of asceticism. They knew repentance before as something that was necessary and a duty; now, in a more perfect manner, they knew its fruit and its reward, *the remission of sins*. Before, they could preach the approaching of the Kingdom of Heaven, but now they could witness concerning its actual appearance before them and within their hearts.

In addition, the Lord foretold His suffering and death to the Apostles also very early in His ministry, repeating it many times and in great detail. Sometimes, He concealed this prophecy with figurative language; for example, when He said to the Jews: *Destroy this temple, and in three days I will raise it up*. When they heard these words, they thought of the physical Temple, *But He was speaking of the temple of His body*. However, it must be said that often His parables were as easily decipherable as His plain speech: *For as Jonah was three days and three nights in the belly of the great fish, so will the Son of Man be three days and three nights in the heart of the Earth*. But this was not enough. This is not how He spoke to His Apostles in the presence of the crowd, but to the Apostles directly He spoke often without any parables, clearly, exactly, in detail. For example: *Behold, we are going up to Jerusalem, and all things that are written by the Prophets concerning the Son of Man will be accomplished. For He will be delivered to the Gentiles and will be mocked and insulted and spit upon. They will scourge Him and kill Him. And the third day He will rise again.* Can anything be clearer than that? Is it even possible to misunderstand these words? And honestly, can you tell me that they didn't understand Him fully? *(Luke 18:31-33)*

The holy Evangelist anticipated this objection; and so, he assures us with a careful choice of words that they truly did not understand Christ. *But they understood none of these things; this saying was hidden from them, and they did not know the things which were spoken.* Mark adds that one time, when they heard the Lord speaking of His Resurrection, the Apostles were so confused about the meaning of His words, that they stopped and began to argue amongst themselves about the possible interpretation. *So they kept this word to themselves, questioning what rising from the dead meant.* And so, it is clear that it occurred no earlier than after the Resurrection of the Lord: *And He opened their understanding, that they might comprehend the Scriptures...[that] it was necessary for the Christ to suffer and to rise from the dead on the third day.* *(Luke 18:34, Mark 9:10, Luke 24:45-46)*

I'm afraid that, in spite of such obvious proof in the Gospel, the reality of the close-mindedness of the Apostles before the Resurrection, and the suddenness of their illumination at the mere sight of the Resurrection Christ, might be too much for some to swallow. Oh, if only the Lord would open my understanding as well! I would say something instructive, and you would hear something illuminating about how the mind opens through the light of the resurrected Christ and through faith in Him!

The word of God calls the mind an eye, it calls knowledge vision, and ignorance blindness, as in this example: *For judgment I have come into this world, that those who do not see may see, and that those who see may be made blind.* It is clear that the coming of Christ into the world made no one physically blind, but many were revealed to be blind in their mind. Let us then follow this meta- *(John 9:39)* phor, used in the Scriptures, that equates the state and action of the mind with the state and action of the eye.

The eye sees things at least in part due to the qualities of the actual things. For example: the light is visible in brightness. But part of what the eye sees is due to the way the eye is structured. For example, the eyes of the blind man, as they were being slowly opened, at first saw *men like trees, walking*, and after complete healing, *he... saw everyone clearly*. Vision also depends on the interaction between viewer and thing viewed. For example: you see one thing in the light of the moon, and an entirely different thing in the light of the sun. In a similar way, the spiritual eye sees spiritual objects, or, to put it a different way, the mind understands them, partly because of the nature of the things viewed. Thus, for example, "since the creation of the world His invisible attributes are clearly seen" by the mind (Romans 1:20). Partly, the vision of our spiritual eyes depends on our own inner state. For example, the childish mind sees objects more sensually, superficially, without much connection or synthesis of ideas, while the educated mind sees more profoundly into the essence of things, revealing their interconnectedness and inherent order. Finally, our inner vision also depends on the relation between the mind and the objects of the world, which could be either natural, or supernatural, or belonging to the world we live in, which is an admixture of the sensual and the spiritual, or, lastly, purely spiritual or even divine, as it is written: *In Your light shall we see light*.

Mark 8:24
Mark 8:25

Psalm 35:10

The nature of the physical eye limits its vision only to the visible spectrum, so that it loses its power of vision in dim light and also becomes blind in the presence of too much light. On the other hand, the nature of the mind, which is a spiritual tool, is incomparably broader and more subtle. The human mind can become a kind of nocturnal bird that only sees in the darkness, and for whom any kind of light is blindness. Or, it can become like an animal that hunts only in the light of the moon. Or, it can act, as is right for human beings — in the light of the sun doing its proper work, examining all the many beauties of the world. If it goes down too far, it becomes entrapped in the world of the senses, but if it rises, it becomes capable of seeing divine light, becoming purified and ready to accept the light of God.

Whoever desires to see spiritual realities, without a doubt, will not content himself with merely opening his physical eyes and lighting a candle. The more exalted the object of vision, the more exalted should be the state of the mind and the light that helps illumine that object. Consequently, to see divine realities, a divine light is needed, and so, the mind must be conformed to that divine reality and light. *In Your light, O Lord, shall we see light.*   Psalm 35:10

The word of God, the mysteries of the Kingdom of God, the salvific teaching and salvific works of Christ, without a doubt, are divine objects. Consequently, in order to see these clearly and correctly, man needs divine light, the light of Christ, the light of the Holy Spirit, and the opening of his mind by the power of this light. Until this occurs in a person, though he listens to the word of God, or even sees it in action, he still will not understand the fullness of its dimensions, since his spiritual eye is still mired in the lower light of the sensual (the natural), and can only see in this natural light. This is why the Apostles, though they saw the Resurrection of the son of the widow of Nain with their physical eyes, could not yet raise their contemplative mind to answer the question: *what rising from the dead meant.*   Mark 9:10

This is also why the Lord said to the Apostles, *I still have many things to say to you, but you cannot bear them now.* When, O Lord,   John 16:12
will they be able to bear Your words and understand Your works? He answers, *When He, the Spirit of truth, has come, He will guide you into all truth.* But what prevents this Spirit from coming more   John 16:13
quickly? Again, the Gospel answers, *The Holy Spirit was not yet given, because Jesus was not yet glorified.*   John 7:39

Finally, He is risen. If before, all that was divine in Him was concealed in His humanity, from this moment on, all that was human in Him rises up to the divine. And so, His humanity is revealed, filled not with hidden, but evident, divine light, and it pours out onto all who are around Him. The God-man is revealed as the Sun of all mankind, and He begins to part the clouds and the darkness that covered it before. His divine light strikes the eyes that have been opened by faith in His Resurrection, and it drives those eyes toward contemplation. Then, it opens the eyes even more, or rather raises them to a new, heavenly, divine vision — the knowledge of the word of God and the works of God. *And He opened their understanding.*

Luke 24:45

If this opening of the mind, or spiritual illumination, appears sudden or quick, this not only should not seem strange, but entirely appropriate to any light, especially spiritual light. When the sun rises, it suddenly reveals an entire world of various beauties. Is it so strange, then, that the light of grace, the light of the Holy Spirit, whose action in the heart the Apostle Peter compares to a light *that shines in a dark place, until the day dawns and the morning star rises in your hearts*, quickly and suddenly reveals the limitless region of spiritual knowledge? The divine light works the same way as physical light — just as there is a natural dawn and midday, so there is a spiritual analogue. For the Apostles, the bright dawn began at the moment when the Lord *breathed on them, and said to them, 'Receive the Holy Spirit.'*. The full light of day revealed itself to them when the Holy Spirit descended on them in tongues of fire.

2 Peter 1:19

John 20:22

However, if our eyes are still too weak to fully enjoy the light through which the resurrected Lord opens our minds, let us for a moment turn our gaze to its opposite, - the darkness, all the easier to help us come to love the truly miraculous light to which we are called. Look at how at the same moment when faith in the Resurrected One opens the minds of the Apostles, the Jews' continued lack of faith in Him imprisons their minds in a palpable darkness that is incredibly base. What do they think when others speak of the Resurrection of the Lord? *This saying is commonly re-*

ported among the Jews until this day. What saying is this? The saying given by the chief priests to the guards of the Lord's tomb: *His disciples came at night and stole Him away while we slept.*

    Matthew 28:15

    Matthew 28:13

And so, this saying rushed through the Jewish community. Could they have actually believed it? Is it possible? How could you possibly steal His body when the tomb was surrounded by soldiers? Well, they were sleeping, said the Jews. A professional band of soldier-guards fell asleep?! Yes, so the Jews say. Every single one of these soldiers fell asleep? Yes. Is it possible that not a single one of them woke up, especially since it would be necessary to move a massive stone to even get inside? This would have required several people, and they could not have done it without making a great deal of noise. No, not one of them woke up.

    see Mark 16:14

But wait, who is the witness that the body was stolen? The guards. Wait, what? The same guards who slept and didn't wake up? These are supposed to witness to something that happened while they slept, something that they didn't see or hear? Who could have had the gumption to tell such a fairy tale? The unbelieving Jews. Who could have had the madness to believe it? The faithless ones. Let us also ask how it could be possible that the disciples of Jesus, who ran away at the first sign of His impending danger, suddenly decided to perform a brazen and hopeless act — the theft of the dead body of their Teacher from a sealed tomb that was surrounded by a professional detail of guards, according to official command? But unbelief doesn't discuss this; it rushes to spread everywhere the foolish words that it prefers because it pampers its own lack of faith.

However, since it became known that a successful theft was performed under the very noses of a professional guard detail, from under the very seal of the government (and the thieves are even well-known men!), were the guards and thieves both not remanded to the justice of the courts? Not in the least. The head of the guard detail doesn't care, the guards are without remorse, and the alleged thieves remain in Jerusalem for no less than eight days, and not one of the heretofore strict rulers of the Jews demands that they be convicted for such a brazen crime! Is it even possible that after all this, the fairy tales concerning the body of Jesus continued to spread among the Jews as something worthy of attention? Indeed, it is possible, because the mind that has become hardened in unbelief, like a nocturnal bird, can only see in the darkness of unbelief. Such a mind only loves its own delusions, and it flees from the light of truth, which burns its eyes. *This saying is commonly reported among the Jews until this day.*

Matthew 28:15

O Christians! The resurrected Christ opened the minds of the Apostles, and through faith, He illumined them with divine light, not only for their own sakes, but so that they could also open our minds, and so that we, through faith, would become sons of the light. He even allowed the foolish saying of the Jews to reach our own ears, for that only displays the extreme blindness of the unbelieving Jews, so that we may truly fear such unbelief. Do not say with Thomas, *Unless I see... I will not believe.* Instead, remember the words of the Lord, if you believe, *you will see greater things than these. While you have the light, believe in the light, that you may become sons of light.*

John 20:25

John 1:50
John 12:36

May faith and love attract you to the Light of life that shines from the tomb. May this Light open your minds to the knowledge of the mysteries of your salvation, and your hearts to the experience of the Kingdom of God, which is within you. May Eden and Heaven also be revealed in the heart that is open to the Kingdom of God. May we not shut ourselves off from ourselves through sin and lack of faith in all that the Key of David opens for us. Amen.

16

Homily on Holy Pascha (1826)

Christ is risen!

Having said this, what more can I say? Everything is already said.

Do you need to establish your faith, to create hope, to arouse life, to illumine with wisdom, to raise your prayer on high, to call down grace, or to destroy calamities, death, and evil? To give content to your life, to make blessedness not simply a dream but a reality, or to make glory not simply an apparition but the eternal lightning of the eternal light that illumines everyone without striking them down? The single miraculous phrase, "Christ is risen!" has enough power to cause all of that.

If Christ is not risen, your faith is futile, says one of the most active preachers of the faith. What a horrifying thought! But the more terrifying it is, the more instructive is the opposite truth: since Christ is risen, then our faith is unconquerable and salvific. The pagan believes as well, but only in dead divinities or even created things, while he himself is also mortal — how can faith be strong if divinity is mortal? How can it give life when it is dead? The Jew

1 Corinthians 15:17

believes in the living God, but only according to the writings of the Law, which kill the sinner but are incapable of resurrecting him. What can one expect of this faith other than what we see? It killed the Christ-killing people of Judea, it scattered their bones all over the known world, and it destroyed itself so fully that neither the Jew nor his faith have any hope except in Christianity.

Some wise men of ancient times, who came to understand the foolishness of paganism, but who had not passed into the sanctum of divine truth, invented a faith in an unknown supreme being — God — and they even raised an altar to Him. Perhaps such an altar might be not useless even for some modern wise men, because it doesn't require any serious sacrifices. However, if God is unknown, then how one must serve Him is also not known. And in this case, can any of our service be pleasing to Him or salvific to us? Therefore, any faith founded on ignorance is destroyed by that same ignorance.

We, Christians, believe in a living God, according to the law *of the Spirit of life in Christ Jesus [who] has made me free from the law of sin and death*. We know—this is what we dare to assert, together with the Apostle—*whom [we] have believed and [are] persuaded that He is able to keep what [we] have committed to Him*. What does it mean that we *are persuaded*? First all, we are persuaded by the Resurrection of the One *we have believed*. If He resurrected, raised, and enthroned His faith, in His own person, though it was buried in a tomb and descended into Hades, then we are persuaded of His power to both establish, preserve, and justify our faith.

If in this life only we have hope in Christ, we are of all men the most pitiable. Those who do not believe, find for themselves in their unbelief the advantage that they can enjoy the pleasures of this world without care, and to take advantage of the goodwill of this world. However, it must be said that this advantage is not enviable, as it is no less than a curse, for when it is said, "of all men we are the most pitiable," the people here mentioned are all those who are unbelievers, and so all of them are more or less pitiable,

Romans 8:2

2 Timothy 1:12

2 Timothy 1:12

1 Corinthians 15:19

or even accursed. However, if someone were to remove from us, who believe in Christ, the conviction that the Resurrection occurred, then truly we would be the most accursed of all people. The Lord said, *If you were of the world, the world would love its own.* Consequently, the world, if it does not always persecute those who are not of the world, that is, Christians, it does always hate us. Lovers of the world seek pleasures; Christians either reject pleasures outright, and so suffer their absence, or, if they allow themselves some pleasures, they must suffer later through repentance. However, the world deludes itself, if it thinks that it will make us despair through its evil pleasure. *John 15:19*

If everything that this world considers valuable is lost, we have lost nothing at all, for our hope is founded on something deeper than this world, and so it is established in a higher place. *Christ is risen from the dead, and has become the first fruits of those who have fallen asleep. If the Spirit of Him who raised Jesus from the dead dwells in you, He who raised Christ from the dead will also give life to your mortal bodies through His Spirit who dwells in you.* Do you need anything more for your perfect hope? If you do, know this: we already have everything that is promised to replace the present in the future: *1 Corinthians 15:20* / *Romans 8:11*

> But God, who is rich in mercy, because of His great love with which He loved us, ⁵ even when we were dead in trespasses, made us alive together with Christ (by grace you have been saved), ⁶ and raised us up together, and made us sit together in the heavenly places in Christ Jesus, ⁷ that in the ages to come He might show the exceeding riches of His grace in His kindness toward us in Christ Jesus. *Ephesians 2:4-7*

When the *great love of God*, through the Resurrection of Christ, indestructibly establishes us in Christ, and consoles us with perfect faith, then what must our heart feel, if our crude sensuality has not yet made it incapable of sensing spiritual influences? What else except that same love of God, by which God, the eternal Sun, shines for us, arousing in us love for Himself? *For the* *Ephesians 2:4-7 love of Christ compels us, because we judge thus: that if One died for all, then all died.* And in a different place, as soon as the Apostle says it was Christ Jesus "who died, and furthermore is also risen, who is even at the right hand of God, who also makes intercession for us," he immediately declares, in irrepressible ecstasy, *Who shall separate us from the love of Christ?*.

Truly, according to the words of Love Himself, "Greater love has no one than this, than to lay down one's life for his friends" (John 15:13). But Love without measure came to love us while we were still His enemies, even laying down His life for our sake, even a death on the cross. Can we be so ungrateful and insensitive to prevent Love, resurrected for our sake, from resurrecting our own love for Him?

I will not further elucidate the many miracles that occur from the single miraculous phrase, "Christ is risen!" If it raises up within us a holy love for God, which we constantly kill inside ourselves through a sinful love of the world and the flesh, then that miracle is enough for the completion of today's joy and for the revelation of all other miracles in their own time. If the risen Christ has aroused your heart with sweet desire and a certain hidden sense of His divine presence during this feast day, as He did to the disciples on the road to Emmaus, then it would not be a vain word, and certainly not a mere convention, to greet each other with the words of the Apostles to the travelers returning from Emmaus: *The Lord is risen indeed!*

Indeed He is risen!

Amen!

17

Homily on Holy Pascha (1827)

Christ is risen!

God has allowed us to see another one of these triumphant days, this crown of all feasts. Blessed is the one who has placed all times and seasons into His own power.

Truly, the day of the Resurrection of Christ is the king of all days. Just as the subjects of a good king receive safety, peace, and justice from him, so the good power of the day of the Resurrection of Christ gives all other days safety and peace, for otherwise we would, *through fear of death, [be] all [our] lifetime subject to bondage*. It gives all other days justice as well, for every day of birth, life, and death, for each of us, would have been worthy of a curse if they were not all blessed by the day of the Resurrection of Christ. Perhaps it was for this reason, by the way, that the light of the un-blessed days faded at the moment of the death of Christ, for from His death and resurrection, a new light of blessed days arose, that miraculously illumined both all the ages to come and all the ages that had already passed.

Hebrews 2:15

Yes, even the past, for Abraham, so many centuries before the Resurrection of Christ, enjoyed the light not of his own times, but this day, which he awaited in faith, as Jesus Christ Himself said to the Jews: *Your father Abraham rejoiced to see My day, and he saw it and was glad.* He saw this much-desired day especially when *he received [Isaac] in a figurative sense*, after Isaac had been brought as a sacrifice of the heart for three days through intention, after Abraham had actually placed Isaac on the altar, on top of the wood for the burning, under the sacrificial knife, and under the death-bearing hand. That is, he received him once again alive, as a sign of the coming Resurrection of Christ from the dead, after three days, after a visible sacrifice on the cross and an internal immolation.

John 8:56
Hebrews 11:19

In order for the day of the Resurrection of Christ to illumine the future days and ages, observe how the very Sun of righteousness Himself—Jesus Christ—gives them an undying light. For He said to the sons of the light, the Apostles, *I will see you again and your hearts will rejoice, and your joy no one will take from you.* If no one can steal this joy, then evidently it must shine for all future days and ages.

John 16:22

O Christians, children of the light, even if lesser children! O, if only this day, which Abraham was joyful to see, and which brought endless joy to the Apostles, would bring us, every new year, an incremental increase of spiritual light, and a new confirmation in the joy of salvation!

Perhaps it might seem to some that I ask for too much, even demand it, when I express my hope that the joy and light of the Resurrection of Christ will always grow inside us. After all, the joy and light of Pascha will always come to us in the same form (the same liturgical cycle), and so, how can they ever increase in us or reach the fullness of power that the Apostles felt? The Apostles heard the promise of joy and saw the Resurrected One in person after all.

Listen then to my justification; I hope to be justified quickly. Listen to the promise of joy given to the Apostles, and through them to all of us: *I will see you again and your hearts will rejoice.* In our understanding, this is what He should have said, "You will see me, and your hearts will rejoice." For we rejoice when *we* see the One we love; while the fact that He sees us perhaps has no inner effect on us at all, for when we do not see Him, then our hearts have no reason to rejoice. And yet, in contrast to that, the Lord said this, as though everything depended on His seeing the Apostles, and as though there would be no special difference in their seeing Him or not.

John 16:22

Well, what is the Wisdom of God saying to us through this expression? The fact that just as the light of this visible world comes from the sun, which is the eye of this world, so also the light of the soul and the joy of the heart comes from the eyes of the Son of God, Jesus Christ, who is the Sun of the invisible world. It means that as the sun, when it rises and looks at the world, gives beneficial light to earthly beings, as much as each of them is capable of receiving it, so also the God-man Jesus, when He looks at the soul and heart (especially after He ascended into the true spring and new morning of the world in His humanity, which, having been raised up through sufferings, became, so to speak, transparent for the indwelling of the divinity, as though the wounds on the cross were open doors for the divine light), He gives grace-filled light by His presence to souls and joy to hearts, as much as their spiritual abilities allow them to receive, that is, depending on the amount of faith and love they possess.

The pleasure we have at the light of the sun doesn't depend at all on whether we actually see the movement of the sun or not. Even the one who doesn't raise his eyes to the sun or squint to see its movement still enjoys its light. Even the one who sits in shadows or stands under a cloud still enjoys the light of the sun. In the same way, the pleasure at the Lord's light, and our joy in the Lord, are not attached to the actual vision of Christ appearing before our earthly eyes. Even someone who does not dare raise his gaze to the height of His glory, in humility, and even someone who stands under the cloud of faith, and someone who rests in the shade of hope — all these can find pleasure in the spiritual light and heavenly joy. In fact, sometimes it is even safer to enjoy the light thus than to see the extraordinary vision of the light, for which we must have an eagle's eye, lest we be blinded by the excess of light.

And so, it is true, with reference to joy in the Lord, everything depends on whether or not the resurrected Lord looks at us; it does not at all depend on whether or not we see Him with our physical eyes. The most important thing is for the resurrected Lord to see us not only with the undimmed eye of His omnipresence and omniscience, which pierces all things, and from which even the darkest thought in the depths of Hell cannot hide, but also that He see us through the bright and light-giving eye of grace, the fiery eye of love by which He looks at all without difference, but through His own choice, as He looked after His Resurrection at His myrrh-bearing women and Apostles. All the same, it should be said that this choice, in His mercy, does not exclude anyone, unless we exclude our own selves.

He does not wait for us to seek the gaze of His grace; but, preceding us, He seeks among us those on whom He might look with the gaze of grace, and so He shows us the disposition that we must aspire to so that His gaze may in the future fall upon us. *On this one will I look: on him who is poor and of a contrite spirit,* Isaiah 66:2 *and who trembles at my word.* If you can do no more, seek only to have meekness, contrition of spirit, and fear of God, and the Lord will look at you, according to the Law of inheritance that He has Himself declared for all of us. Then, just as with the Apostles, He will fulfill the promise He gave them, and to all of you in their persons: *You will see me, and your hearts will rejoice.*

John 16:22

In order to come to believe in these truths through undoubting experience, let us look at the first and the nearest communicants of the joy of the Resurrection of Christ. Their various experiences give us many firm proofs of the truth of this much-desired event, and just as many true instructions for our salvific and blessed participation in it. Was their joy in the Resurrection directly tied to their physical vision of the Resurrected One? Did the deprivation of this physical vision lead to a lessening of their joy? Do not their lives prove the exact opposite? You might remind me of the words of John: *Then the disciples were glad when they saw the Lord*. Yes, this is true; however, even before them, did not the myrrh-bearers rejoice with an even greater joy, though they did not yet see Him? *So they went out quickly from the tomb with fear and great joy, and ran to bring His disciples word.* [John 20:20] [Matthew 28:8]

Thomas thought that he had a right to demand a sighting, and he received the answer to his demand—yes, it is true that this led not only to joy, but to ecstasy; however, did the fact that he saw Him make him especially joyful? The One who granted the vision believed otherwise; He rebuked Thomas through His appearance, and He blessed those who did not see. *Because you have seen Me, you have believed. Blessed are those who have not seen and yet have believed.* And to be blessed, without a doubt, is much greater than sudden ecstasies and is more perfect that simple joy. Even the Apostle Peter, an eye-witness of the Resurrected One, who knew the value of this vision, still ascribes the greatest degree of joy to those who believe without seeing: *Whom having not seen you love. Though now you do not see Him, yet believing, you rejoice with joy inexpressible and full of glory, receiving the end of your faith—the salvation of your souls.* [John 20:29] [1 Peter 1:8-9]

In this way, I hope I have demonstrated that the rising of the internal light and spiritual joy, contained in the Resurrection of Christ, can act with as much power in us, though we have not seen Him, as it did on *those who from the beginning were eyewitnesses*. And if their experiences show us that this joy was not only preserved in them without fading, according to the promise, then this quality of permanence proves that this joy must only [Luke 1:2] [John 16:22] grow and become more perfect in them. And so, this only proves that it is not too much of us to ask, even demand, that this joy not only not fade within us but always increase like the light of morning until the fullness of the day of our illumination by the Holy Spirit—the endless day of the Kingdom of Christ. And so, let us look once more at the experiences of the eyewitnesses of the Resurrection of Christ.

When the disciples were filled with joy at seeing the Lord, this was not yet a high degree or a perfected form of joy, for it was still mixed with lack of faith, as we find out when reading the Gospel according to Luke. They still needed more physical proofs of the Resurrection to fully believe: *But while they still did not believe for joy, and marveled, He said to them, 'Have you any food here?' And He took it and ate in their presence.* But when they, having been parted from the Lord after His Ascension, *worshipped Him and returned to Jerusalem with great joy,* can you not see that the joy in them had become much more exalted and more firm than before? For this separation from the Source of their joy did not lessen their joy, but made it even greater than before! Finally, examine how the same Apostles *departed from the presence of the council, rejoicing that they were counted worthy to suffer shame for His name.* This joy is even more exalted and powerful; in fact, it is truly indestructible when neither enmity, nor persecution, nor dishonor, nor wounds can damage it.

Luke 24:41, 43

Luke 24:52

Acts 5:41

And so, I will return to my original desire: Oh, if only the joy of this day would become for us a joy in life that always grows, like a life of ageless eternal youth, like the life of Heaven!

But how can we do this? This you will probably ask me. How can we do this? How can we make our joy, which in its principle is eternal, not short-lived? How can we make our joy, which in its consequences is eternal and limitless, grow and become stronger within us on the way to its own endlessness and eternity? It seems to me that to do this is less difficult than living in any other way. All you need to do is not hinder divine joy, do not cast it out, do not squelch it, and it will continue, grow, and become perfected in and of itself, until it finally becomes blessedness.

In the book of Joel, there is an interesting expression about how people lose their joy and become subjected to sorrows and calamities: *The vine has dried up, and the fig tree has withered; the pomegranate tree, the palm tree also, and the apple tree — all the trees of the field are withered; surely joy has withered away from the sons of men.* Pure joy is a noble and pure maiden who has as her constant companion an undisturbed conscience. She can only bear to be in the company of those whose deeds are unpolluted, whose words are meek, whose intentions are pure and exalted. As soon as you allow yourselves any sinful actions, any vain or frivolous works, any impure or debased intentions, she immediately notices it, and her nobility is ashamed, and her chastity is embarrassed, and she runs away and hides from you. If the crude and mad joy of the world takes her place, so much the worse for you. The justice of Heaven sends a curse on all sources of earthly joy, for the sake of the insult done to heavenly joy. *The vine has dried up, and the fig tree has withered; the pomegranate tree, the palm tree also, and the apple tree—all the trees of the field are withered; surely joy has withered away from the sons of men.*

Joel 1:12

Joel 1:12

O sons of men! Or better yet, sons of God in Christ! Let us not shame our heavenly joy or the life in God through an impure life or the deeds of crude sensuality, and our God will put *gladness in our hearts* that is even better than those who have *the fruit of their wheat, and wine, and oil...increase.* And may no one take away our joy in the resurrected and eternally living Jesus Christ, our Lord. Amen.

Psalm 4:8

18

Homily on Holy Pascha (1842)

Christ is risen!

In triumphant fashion, the Church of Christ sounded this most exalted of all greetings: *In the beginning was the Word, and the Word was with God, and the Word was God*, and so on. And since we know this custom of the Church — to illumine the mystery of the day through a reading of the Gospel, and to give us a subject for reverent contemplation and spiritual instruction, then what must I do now?

Should I try to raise your soul from the Earth, to lift it up above the sun and stars, to lead it to the Heaven of heavens, past the low and high ranks of Angels, all the way to the highest points of the created world, to the place where there is no time, because that is the place of endless and indivisible eternity, where space itself disappears in infinity, and from where, with a glance back, one can easily say that Solomon's words were not an exaggeration, but rather an understatement, that *the entire world before You is like a small additional weight on scales, and like a drop of dew early in the morning that falls on the ground*? Should I demand that all

John 1:1

(Wis. of Sol. 11:23)

of you stand still in contemplation, together with the Evangelist John, higher even than the Prophet Habakkuk stood, since the Prophet gazed at the Son of God in His incarnation, while the Evangelist gazed at Him in the Mystery of His pre-eternal Birth?

Should I speak with you about the beginning, about the most exalted meaning of this word, of the beginning of all beginnings, as David calls it, of the beginning that far precedes our own time and even time itself, of the beginning from which eternity itself begins, but which is not limited by any beginning, nor any possible end point? Should I find the words to help you better understand and speak of that *Word*, which not only the human, but the angelic mind cannot comprehend, and which no tongue can properly elucidate, the *Word* that spoke singly and that the Father of the Word eternally speaks into existence or birth, and who Himself speaks the existence of all creation, not in a way that we can hear or understand, but essentially into being?

Should I more simply retell the most exalted word of God the Word, that *in the beginning was the Word*, that is, *the only begotten Son, who is in the bosom of the Father*, that by His birth He was not separated from God the Father, but is one in essence with the Father and the Holy Spirit, that the Word was God, that is, that the Name of God in that same true sense that it belongs to God the Father belongs equally to the Son of God, just as it does to the Holy Spirit? Should I explain how in the three divine Hypostases there is only one God in essence, that by this hypostatic Word of God everything was created without divine subtraction, everything that is heavenly and earthly, visible and invisible? That in Him is the source of life or the source of life for all that lives? Especially those who live a spiritual and eternal life, that this source of life always was, and is, and will be the light for mankind that shone for them in Paradise? That this light did not completely fade for them on Earth, was not put out by the darkness of paganism (though the pagans did not see it and did not accept it), and that it showed a sign of itself in the Law of Moses? That this light dawned in the Prophets, until finally, like

John 1:8

the rising of the sun and the coming of day, this light came in the incarnate Word, with the full light of truth, with His life-giving and miraculous power, in His life, preaching, actions, and even in His willing suffering and death, and the more so in His Resurrection? *We beheld His glory, the glory as of the only begotten of the Father, full of grace and truth.*

_{John 1:14}

Can you see? I have only just begun to speak theology under the direction of holy John the Theologian; and, perhaps, what little I have said is already too brazen because of the paucity of my words, and—do not be angry with me—because of the weakness of your own hearing. After all, among all the God-inspired Evangelists, is it not only the one son of thunder who so triumphantly sounds the good news of the supra-heavenly glory of God the Word?

When we listen to the sounds of thunder, we do not understand them as exactly and distinctly as the Son of Thunder once understood the mystical voice of seven thunders; however, we do feel that they tell us of the greatness of God. In a similar way, when we hear the exalted language of St. John about God the Word, though we do not completely understand it with our rational mind (because of the weakness of our minds and the mysterious nature of the subject itself), we can still feel that through these words the majesty of our Lord Jesus Christ, divine in essence, salvific for us, is imparted to us. And this is enough.

One can wonder and be amazed at how it happened that our wise teacher, the holy Church, allotted such a difficult lesson for this day of celebration. Would it not be more appropriate to include references about the Resurrection from the Gospels on this day? Would it not make sense to inspire and nourish joy on this day of joy? Was not joy the first child of the Resurrection, though at the same time it was accompanied by fear from the sudden appearance of miracles? For having come to see the tomb, and instead having heard the good news of the Lord's Resurrection,

Matthew 28:1

they went out quickly from the tomb with fear and great joy, and ran to bring His disciples word. Matthew 28:8

Did not the Resurrected One Himself command us to rejoice in the day of the Resurrection? *Behold, Jesus met them, saying, 'Rejoice'!* What happened to the Apostles when they saw the Resurrected Jesus and were assured that it was Him by His wounds from the cross? *Then the disciples were glad when they saw the Lord.* And does not the Church herself admit the mastery of joy on this day above all other days, filling nearly the entire service with triumphant hymnody, with nearly no readings or sermons? Matthew 28:9
John 20:20

I say this to you not to enter into argument with Mother Church concerning her order of services, but to give you a better opportunity to understand that order, all the better to fulfill it.

What was the thought of Mother Church when she decided, amid the joy of the feast, to call her children to the difficult contemplation of the most exalted of truths, or to the most exalted contemplation of the mystery of the truth? Without a doubt, the Church would not have found it appropriate to do so if it brought us to sensual joy, which is corrupted by vanity, frivolity, and noise. And so, if she found it appropriate, then, without a doubt, she did so because our festal joy must be spiritual, pure, peaceful, and exalted, for such a joy not only does not impede conscientious and profound contemplation, but makes a person more capable of exalted contemplation than usual.

The Gospel gives us many examples of this. When the future mother of the Forerunner and the future Mother of God, having seen each other, became joyful with pure joy, and the joy of the righteous Elizabeth then communicated itself to the child in her womb, what was the result of this triple joy? Both mothers came to a state of spiritual ecstasy, and both of them began to prophesy. When Thomas, who was deprived of the joy of the Resurrection for a longer time than the other Apostles because of his lack of faith, suddenly felt that joy overcome him as he touched the wounds of the Resurrected One—how did that joy act within him? It resulted in theology: *Thomas answered and said to Him, 'My Lord and my God'!* And this is perfectly natural, for nothing so directly leads one to the thought of, belief in, and faith concerning the divinity of Jesus Christ as His Resurrection.

John 20:28

And so, we have come to know, somewhat, just what sort of joy our joy must be, so that it might correspond both to the dignity of the subject and the intention of Mother Church. O children of the light-bearing Church! Learn how to use that light that our Resurrected Lord so abundantly pours out on you! If it is not so easy to know how to theologize well, then it seems to me at least not that difficult to know how to rejoice well. Be attentive to yourselves and watch over your hearts earnestly, to make sure that your joy in the feast is spiritual, pure, peaceful, and that it raises up your souls.

When you heard from the wise virgins concerning the moment of the heavenly Bridegroom's coming, at midnight, with candles, you surrounded His bridal chamber. You have dedicated hours of the early morning, stolen from sleep, to prayer, the Gospel, the mysteries, the words of truth. By this, you reveal the signs of spiritual and pure joy. When you kiss one another with the kiss of peace, not ostracizing anyone that approaches you — this is a sign of peaceful joy. When every mouth and every ear is filled with the names of Christ and His Resurrection, I happily admit that this is an expression of joy that raises up your soul to the place where the Resurrected One reigns. Up to this point, it seems to me, everything is good. The holy morning is illumined with the light of holy joy.

But will the day, the evening, the subsequent week, which the Church has dedicated for the joy of the Resurrection, be equally worthy? Will not your spiritual joy soon be swallowed up by sensual enjoyment? Everything that you gathered for your soul in the church, will you lose it all completely outside the church because of your inattentive living? After the vision of the holy, heavenly, and the divine, will you then run to the base spectacles of the world, upon which a toy-object, or even worse, a toy-human, will swallow up the attention of your mind and the movements of your heart with their various portrayals of passions, madness, and sins? Will your time, your honors, and your money then be wasted on trifles when they perhaps could have been given to the poor? Is not this what the Prophet calls the dishonoring of joy? *Surely joy has withered away from the sons of men.* *Joel 1:12*

I beg you and I counsel you, do not dishonor the joy that you so reverently honored in the beginning of the feast. Is it appropriate to turn this joy, which was won for us through sacrifice and suffering, into a game or an amusement? *For indeed Christ, our Passover, was sacrificed for us. Therefore, let us keep the feast, not with old leaven, nor with the leaven of malice and wickedness, but with the unleavened bread of sincerity and truth. Let us walk properly, as in* *1 Corinthians 5:7-8* *the day, not in revelry and drunkenness, not in lewdness and lust, not in strife and envy. But put on the Lord Jesus Christ.* *Romans 13:13-14*

He has enough light and incorruptible joy for all and for everyone, so that no one would ever feel the need to pursue a delusive joy, to seek food in corruption for the immortal soul. Seek joy always in its purest source: *Rejoice in the Lord always. Again I will say, rejoice!* *Philippians 4:4*

19

Homily on Paschal Vespers (1844)

Then the disciples were glad when they saw the Lord
(John 20:20).

To see the Lord, without a doubt, is an incomparable joy. The Angels in Heaven do not even know a higher blessedness than to see the Lord.

The disciples' joy in seeing the resurrected Lord was especially powerful because before this joy, they had been suddenly plunged into an abyss of sorrow, and now from that abyss of sorrow, they are just as suddenly raised to a level of joy greater than ever before. As great as their joy was when, in the divine words and miraculous acts of the Lord Jesus, they began to *behold His glory, the glory as of the only begotten of the Father,,* and when they *rejoiced for all the glorious things that were done by Him,* so much greater was their sorrow when He was betrayed into the hands of His enemies, when He was convicted, dishonored, tortured, and killed, and when He only received an honorable burial because of unexpected compassion, and when even in the tomb, He was pursued by His enemies. But the more profound and dark this

John 1:14
Luke 13:17

sorrow, the more triumphant the joy that once again shone in its wake, when in their secret gathering (for they were afraid), through the closed doors, *Jesus came and stood in their midst.* Now, He was triumphant over death, and, consequently, over all who stood in enmity against Him and His followers; now, He had assumed all authority in Heaven and on Earth; now He brought the Holy Spirit; now He truly began the Kingdom of Heaven on Earth, which before He had only announced as imminent. *John 20:19*

And we, today, continue this joy of the first disciples of Christ, for we also are the disciples of Christ, even if we are, perhaps, the last of them, and even if we are more so the last in terms of our unworthiness rather than our historical time. Can we not also see the resurrected Lord, so that we might also rejoice with complete joy? Or, if that be not possible, is it even possible for us to rejoice in Him with complete joy?

To this last question we have a consoling answer from the lips of the Lord Himself. When Thomas, in spite of the obvious eye-witness accounts of the Resurrection, did not want to believe without seeing the resurrected Lord, then the Lord, though He condescended to this brazen demand, also praised those who do not demand to see, for *Blessed are those who have not seen and yet have believed.* *John 20:29*

What a blessed good fortune for us! We can believe in the resurrected Lord without seeing Him, and still we can be blessed. Consequently, we can have the fullness of joy, for blessedness is, by definition, complete joy. The Apostle Peter, in his epistle, speaks exactly of this joy that belongs to those who have believed without seeing, and he speaks of this joy not only as a potential joy, but as something that truly belongs to Christians: *Whom [that is, Jesus] having not seen, you love. Though now you do not see Him, yet believing, you rejoice with joy inexpressible and full of glory.* *1 Peter 1:8*

Brethren! How short is the road to prosperity! How easy it is to become blessed! Not having seen Christ, all you must do is believe in Him, love Him, and rejoice; then, you will be blessed!

But just as we cannot fail to admit that to become worthy of the sight of the One we believe in must raise the joy of the faithful even higher, so also we cannot immediately reject another question: can we, on the day of the Resurrection, be found worthy of attaining the vision of the Resurrected One, just as the Apostles did, though not immediately, *the same day at evening*? Let us not dare to demand this stubbornly, as did Thomas, nor let us threaten loss of faith for any denial of such sight, because such a threat endangers no one but the one making the threat.

John 20:19

But is there no one to whom we might turn with a humble request, as the Greeks did to Philip, *Sir, we wish to see Jesus*? To whom else can we turn except to our Mother Church? And do you hear? She has already answered your desire, and not only does she promise us a potential vision of the Resurrected One, but she announces it as definite. She sings, "Having beheld the Resurrection of Christ, let us worship the Holy Lord Jesus." If we have seen the Resurrection, then we have seen the Resurrected One, because the Resurrection is only visible in the One who rose again. If we understand that the Mother Church first and foremost speaks of her worthy and perfected children, and through their mouths speaks the truth with conviction, ", "we have seen the Resurrection," then for us, who are imperfect and unworthy, all that remains is at least to hope that we may receive this as well, if we zealously labor to become worthy and perfected.

John 12:21

Lest we think the Church's words concerning the vision of the Resurrection seem to contradict the apostolic word concerning faith without seeing, I will endeavor to explain.

It is one thing when we demand *to see* (in cases where there is enough good reason to have faith) as a kind of deposit to help us believe in the future. This is inappropriate to the essence and dignity of faith, just as it is in society: if someone requires a deposit in advance, he is not trustworthy. He is simply brazen. This state is almost the same as unbelief, though, perhaps it is not so different from a desire to have faith. This is not what is approved in Thomas. It is a different thing to believe without seeing, and then to receive sight as a consequence of faith, as a gift, a reward, an encouragement, or as life-giving medicine. This is how the proto-martyr Stephen believed and confessed his faith before his persecutors, subjecting himself to deathly danger for his faith. And for that reason, he then *gazed into Heaven and saw the glory of God, and Jesus standing at the right hand of God.* Acts 7:55

There are also sightings or appearances that were not preceded by desire, not called for by faith, but through which God's providence and mercy sought out future sons of faith. Thus, the Lord appeared in the revealed Heaven to blind, with the light of His vision, the eyes of Saul the persecutor, to then give him a new birth as Paul the Apostle.

It is one thing to see with eye of the body, another to see with spiritual eyes. The Apostle Peter says this about the physical appearance of Christ: *Now you do not see Him, yet believing, you rejoice with joy inexpressible.* However, the Church says this about the spiritual appearance of Christ: "Having beheld the Resurrection of Christ, let us worship the holy Lord Jesus." 1 Peter 1:8

There is, according to the Apostle Paul, *the spirit of revelation* who is given not only to the Prophets and Apostles. We all have inner eyes that can be enlightened, by which our inner man, when he is healthy and spiritually perfect, can look into the invisible Kingdom of grace, just like the outer man can see the natural world with his physical eyes. The Apostle Paul, when speaking in his epistle to the Ephesians to all who are faithful in Christ Jesus, utters this prayer on their behalf: *"That the God of our Lord Jesus Christ, the Father of glory, may give to you the spirit of wisdom and revelation in the knowledge of Him, the eyes of your understanding being enlightened.* From this, it should be evident, first of all, that the gift of seeing the spiritual world can be acquired by every truly faithful person, and, second of all, that one of the ways we can acquire this gift is through prayer. Ephesians 1:17 Ephesians 1:17-18

When the incarnate Son of God was leaving this earthly life, and the Apostles were faced with being deprived of the sweetness of seeing Him with their physical eyes, He promised them that they would be able contemplate him in spiritual grace instead of seeing Him in person: *He who has My commandments and keeps them, it is he who loves Me. And He who loves Me will be loved by My Father, and I will love him and manifest Myself to him.* The experience of those who love the Lord shows that He appears to them, depending on their need and their spiritual ability, sometimes in a form they can see, in His divinized humanity, and sometimes not in visible form, though no less essentially and actually, by giving them His peace, His unutterable and glorious joy, which surpasses all explanation, His inner grace-filled light, the dawn of the never-ending day, and the glimmer of eternal glory.

John 14:21

Now do you see the path to seeing Christ resurrected? Learn His commandments, keep them, and love Him with living and active love, and His Father will come to love you as well, and He will love you as well and will manifest Himself to you. This is as true of a saying as any word of Christ.

Did not all those whom we see in the Gospel as having received the vision of the resurrected Christ follow this path, that is, the path of living love?

After all, what was it that led the Myrrh-bearers to visit the tomb with fragrant oils, when they still did not have enough faith in the Resurrection (since myrrh and fragrant oils are necessary for a dead body, not a resurrected one)? What else, if not their love for Christ, which did not die with His death? It led them to His tomb, as did His love for them, and so, He manifested Himself to them.

What was it that gathered the Apostles and kept them in a single house on the day of Resurrection, though their faith in that Resurrection would only come alive later? Was it fear of the Jews? It is true that this fear forced them to close and lock their doors, but if fear was the primary motivating factor, then they would never have gathered together in the first place, for they would be more easily noticed by their enemies when massed together. Fear would have, on the contrary, dissipated them, sending them on many different paths to personal safety. No! Their love for the Crucified One, which came alive earlier than their faith in him, gathered the scattered sheep of the stricken Shepherd into a single group, and His own love heard the fearful sighs of their love for Him. And so, He manifested Himself to them.

Was it not the same love for the Crucified One that shone forth in the sad glances of the travelers on the road to Emmaus, and in their ceaseless conversation about the events that were so painful to remember, and so dangerous to speak of aloud? Their love found the Beloved One nearby and felt His nearness (even without rational thought) in the fire of their hearts, even before *their eyes were opened and they knew Him...in the breaking of bread.*   Luke 24:31, 35

Brethren! Accept these evangelical words. Seek the resurrected Lord through living faith and active love. Following the example of the apostolic gatherings, seek Him with love in the gatherings of the Church. Like the travelers to Emmaus, seek Him with love through conversations about Him at home, or on the road, with a reverent spirit, or at least have these conversations in your own heart. Like the Myrrh-bearers, seek Him with love in deeds of compassion and philanthropy. And then, He will come to love you as well, He will illumine the eyes of your heart; and in holy contemplation, in pure joy, in the blessedness of a peaceful conscience, He will appear to you Himself. Amen.

20

A Homily on Pascha (1845)

Christ is risen!

We have already spent several festive and triumphant hours celebrating the Crown of all Feasts. A question comes to mind: "How well do we understand the early parts of this feast?" Let us go back in time, from this bright day to the night that has passed. It was a night that began in darkness, but then became no less brilliant than the middle of the day. Let us make sense of what happened.

At midnight, the Church hastened to bring us together for the beginning of the feast. Why? Because the starting time of the feast should be as close as possible to the time of the event being celebrated, that is, Christ's Resurrection. We don't exactly know at what time Christ resurrected. When the Myrrh-bearing women, at the rising of the sun, came to the Lord's tomb, it was already open, and the Angels announced that the Resurrection of Christ had already come to pass. Much earlier, when the Earth shook near the Lord's tomb, the Angel tossed the rock aside from the tomb, terrifying the guards by his appearance and causing them to flee. He made the tomb accessible to the Myrrh-bearers and Apostles.

The Resurrection happened even earlier than that, while the tomb was sealed. This we know because the holy Church, the keeper of Christ's Mysteries, tells us so; however, it happened no earlier than midnight. After all, according to Christ's own words, His had to be a three-day resurrection, and because of this, it had to happen no earlier than the first hours after midnight following Saturday. Within these possible hours, the Church wanted to catch the mystical, wonderful moment of the Resurrection with the first moments of the service of Pascha. This is why we try to celebrate this feast at the same moment as the historical event, just as those celebrating are called to be one with the Creator of the feast.

Just before entering the Church to celebrate Christ's triumphant Resurrection, we sang a hymn remembering Christ's three-day burial. For what reason? First of all, we did this so that the sequence of our remembrances would follow the sequence of historical events. Secondly, before we can fully feel joy, we must first stir up a reverent sorrow in our hearts. This will help us better understand, and more vividly experience, the divine joy of the feast.

We began the feast with a hymn that confesses that Christ's Resurrection is announced by the Angels in Heaven. Then we asked for grace to praise the Resurrection with a pure heart. This song was first proclaimed in the closed altar, while the church was still silent. What does this rite mean? Here we also see a sequence of events. The Angels discovered and glorified Christ's Resurrection before mankind did. When Christ opened the gates of Heaven by the power of His cross, leading the Patriarchs, Prophets, and Old Testament Saints into their rest, this was not visible to those on Earth. It is only by faith that we know of this triumphant procession of the heavenly Church. However, this faith may remain limited, and so we reenact these events in the mysteries of the Church. But if these reenactments fail to move our hearts, we need to ask Christ our God for grace and a pure heart: *Blessed are the pure in heart: for they shall see God.*

Matthew 5:8

After asking the resurrected Christ Himself to help us worthily praise Him, we began to praise Him in this unusual rite. Leaving the altar and the temple, we processed around the church, then stopped before the closed doors of the temple. There, we heard a praise to the Holy Trinity, then the first sung hymn to Christ resurrected. The censer and cross opened the doors of the temple to us, and from the darkness of the outside world we entered into the lit interior of the church. At that moment, we could not help but surrender to the glory of the feast.

These actions we took are so extraordinary that if we did not understand their inherent symbolism, we might think they were inconsistent or strange. What do these symbols represent? We have already addressed this. The earthly Church, in its visible actions, attempts, to the best of its ability, to trace a likeness to the invisible triumph of the heavenly Church.

This is the exalted and ancient rule of the Church's divine services; they must represent the likeness of heavenly realities. This is what the Apostle Paul writes of the Old Testament priests: *[They] serve unto the example and shadow of heavenly things....* The Christian Church is closer to heavenly realities than the Old Testament Church was. The Old Testament Church, for the most part, foreshadowed the descent of the heavenly to the Earth, that is, the incarnation of Christ. The Christian Church, after Christ's descent to Earth, must instead represent how He *ascended up on high, he led captivity captive.* Or rather He freed the prisoners and slaves of Hell and led them out to freedom and blessedness, *You have received gifts for men.* So, through the sacrifice of the cross, He granted mankind the grace-filled gifts of the Holy Spirit.

Hebrews 8:5

Ephesians 4:8

Psalm 68:18

Christ's Resurrection and Ascension did not begin in the tomb. They began in Hell. For after His death on the cross, He was, according to the Paschal hymn, "in the tomb bodily, and in Hell with His soul." "Even to Hell You have descended...and destroyed the darkness dwelling there." The Patriarchs, Prophets, and righteous people of the Old Testament were not weighed down by the darkness of Hell. Still, they could not escape it. They were not able to delight in the fullness of the light of Paradise.

They had a seed of faith in the coming Christ, but only His arrival and the fire of His divine light could ignite their lanterns with true, heavenly life. Their souls, like the wise virgins, waited near the doors of the heavenly palace, but only David's key could unlock the doors. Only the heavenly Bridegroom could walk through the doors and bring the sons of the wedding feast with Him. So, the Savior of the world, after being crucified in the visible world, descended to the very depths of Hell in the invisible world. Then, he ignited the souls of the faithful, leading them out from the entryway of death. He opened the heavens to them, and again in the visible world He revealed the light of the Resurrection.

Have you noticed how the invisible Church united itself to the visible? When we faced the closed doors of the church building in the darkness of night, as though we stood at the gates of Hell, it was as though we stood together with the righteous in Hell before the closed doors of Heaven. The Church instructs us that this is how it was before Christ's Resurrection, and it would have remained thus for eternity if not for Christ's Resurrection. Then, with our praises to the Holy Trinity and the resurrected Christ, the cross and the censer opened the doors of the temple, as though they were the doors of Heaven.

Through these symbols, the Church instruct us that this is how the grace of the Holy Spirit, the Name and power of the resurrected Christ, and our faith and prayer open the doors of Heaven. The burning candles in our hands symbolize not only the light of the Resurrection, but they also remind us of the wise virgins. The candles inspire us to be vigilant, so that with the light of faith, and the oil of myrrh, love, and mercy, we may witness the second and glorious coming of the heavenly Bridegroom in the midnight of all ages. Then, we can hope to find His royal doors open to us.

This is the beautiful mystagogy of the Church! Let us be attentive, brethren, so that we may be faithful to the mysterious guidance of our Mother, the Church.

As we triumph in Christ, who rose again for us, let us not forget, with pain in our hearts, the Christ who was crucified, suffered, died, and was buried for our sake. Otherwise, our joy may become meaningless. Only the one whose inner man is raised with Christ, who retains the hope of the triumphant Resurrection—only such a person receives the full joy of Christ's Resurrection. Only those who participated in the cross, only those who suffer and die with Christ can retain this hope in the triumphant Resurrection. *For if we have been planted together in the likeness of his death, we shall be also in the likeness of his Resurrection. If so be it that we suffer with him, that we may be also glorified together.* Any joy that forgets the cross and death of Christ, which call us to be crucified in the body with our passions and lusts, may find itself in terrible danger. For such joy can turn those who celebrate the Resurrection of Christ into those who crucify Him a second time.

Romans 6:5
Romans 8:17

Following the Angels, we entered the triumph of Christ's Resurrection. We joined the Patriarchs, Prophets, and righteous people of the Old Testament, entering the church as though we were also being led into the heavens. Since that is the case, what should our celebration be like? It should be nearly angelic; it should be worthy of communion with the triumphant Church of the Patriarchs, Prophets, and Saints. It should be worthy of heaven.

Do not think this is impossible because of our weakness. Anyone who celebrates with a pure heart celebrates with the Angels. Anyone who celebrates with love for God and the resurrected Christ, in the spirit of brotherly love, celebrates in communion with the heavenly Church. For the heavens are the Kingdom of divine love. If "he that dwells in love dwells in God" (I John 4:16), then surely he does not dwell lower than Heaven.

However, if it is not difficult to celebrate in communion with the Angels and the heavenly Church, it is even less difficult to fall away and distance ourselves from this communion. Anyone who buries the joy of the spirit with sensual pleasures no longer celebrates with the Angels. Anyone who forgets the heavenly for the sake of the earthly is already far from the heavenly Church. Anyone who does not try to protect his celebrations from sinful works is already not celebrating with the Saints. Anyone who does not preserve and nurture his inner light, letting it go out through negligence, has feeble hope of seeing the opening of the royal doors to Heaven, even if he sees the opening of the royal doors of the sanctuary on Earth.

O Christ our Savior, who is praised by the Angels and the souls of the righteous in Heaven! Help us glorify You in purity of heart on Earth. Amen.

21

Homily on the Ascension (1824)

*And while they looked steadfastly
toward Heaven as He went up, behold, two men
stood by them in white apparel; who also said, 'Men of Galilee,
why do you stand gazing up into Heaven' (Acts 1:10-11)?*

To me it seems strange that you, light-bearing Angels, ask these men of Galilee why they stare up at Heaven. What else should they do but stare at the sky, into which Jesus ascended, the heavens into which their treasure has passed, where their hope and joy has been taken away, where their life has been hidden? If instead they stared at the ground, then it would have been right to ask them why, and indeed it is right to ask all followers of Jesus Christ that look with the eye of their passion down to the Earth—why do you look at the ground? What do you hope to find there after your only Treasure, which was found in Bethlehem, which had passed over the entire land of Judea and Samaria, which had been taken by the hands of thieves in Gethsemane, Jerusalem, and Golgotha, which had been hidden under a stone in the garden of Joseph of

Arimathea, and which was taken and carried away into the treasure-house of Heaven? It was said to you, truly, that *where your treasure is, there your heart will be also*. And so, if your treasure is in the heavens, that is where your heart should be; that is where your gaze, your thoughts, and your desires should be directed.

Matthew 6:21

Two men in white apparel, who immediately after the Ascension of the Lord appeared to the Apostles and asked them why they stared at Heaven, were doubtless themselves inhabitants of Heaven. Therefore, we must not think that this was somehow unpleasant for them, or that they wanted the gaze of the men of Galilee to be directed someplace else! No indeed! They only seek to end the inert wonder of the Apostles: *why do you stand gazing up into Heaven?* Having awoken them from this amazement, they led them to contemplation, and so they instruct the Apostles (and us as well) with what thoughts we must look up into Heaven, following the Ascension of the Lord Jesus:

This same Jesus, who was taken up from you into Heaven, will so come in like manner as you saw Him go into Heaven.

Acts 1:11

Even though our Lord, after His Resurrection, appeared to the Apostles many times, then became invisible—and so, they could become somewhat comfortable with such miraculous events—this time, when He parted from them on the Mount of Olives, He did not simply leave or become invisible, but He ascended visibly above the clouds and only ceased being visible to them because of the incredible height to which He rose. There is no doubt that this manner of departure appeared to them, even after a certain expectation of the miraculous, to be especially unusual and of special importance.

To them, it must have appeared as a vivid fulfillment of His own words, spoken to Mary Magdalene: *I am ascending to My Father and your Father, and to My God and your God.* They had to have concluded that these joyful visits with Him, these instructive conversations with Him, the obvious fact of being in the presence of the God-man, which had lasted for forty days, would end

John 20:17

after this moment. When neither hand nor voice could reach the ascended One, all that was left was to gaze with the eyes, in the hopes of holding on to Him as long as possible. *They looked steadfastly toward Heaven as He went up.* We can imagine what limitless deprivation the Apostles must have felt after the departure of Jesus, who was their entire world. And this limitless deprivation is what the heavenly powers immediately seek to redress. *This same Jesus, who was taken up from you into Heaven, will so come in like manner.*

<small>Acts 1:10</small>

<small>Acts 1:11</small>

O Christian! If you have come to know the Lord Jesus even a little bit, if you have tasted that the Lord is good, then of course, to a greater or lesser degree, you can see how empty the world is without Him. You can feel how empty your heart is without Him. This is how it should be, because everything in the world is *vanity of vanities*, and such vanity cannot fill the heart that Jesus created for righteousness. *For all that is in the world* is *lust*, or an object that attracts lust in its various forms, and since *the world is passing away, and the lust of it*, or, in other words, since the objects that arouse our lust will soon disappear, then no matter how great the world, no matter how varied its good things, no matter how abundant the sources of its pleasures, all of this cannot ever fill the small vessel of the human heart, which, being eternal, can only be filled with eternal life. If, upon feeling such emptiness in created things, you still think that the Lord, who is your truth, your life, your desire, and the fullness of all you desire, is departing from you, hiding Himself, leaving you not only without consolation, but filled with sorrows—not only alone, but among the enemies of your salvation—if your piercing gaze cannot plumb the depth of the heavens, which are closed by clouds, and the unattainable judgments of the Almighty seem to you nothing but uncertainty, then accept from the heavenly authorities this word, filled with power. It can fill your emptiness, soften your sorrow, put an end to your solitude, lighten your darkness, resolve your uncertainty, and give life to your spirit through a nev-

<small>Psalm 33:9</small>

<small>Ecclesiastes 1:2</small>

<small>1 John 2:16-17</small>

er-false and never-fading hope: *This same Jesus, who was taken up from you into Heaven, will so come in like manner.*   Acts 1:11

To this consoling and salvific witness concerning the future coming of the ascended Lord, the heavenly messengers added a certain explanation of how this return will occur. *He will so come in like manner as you saw Him go into Heaven.* They say that the   Acts 1:11
coming of the Lord will be similar to His departing, His Ascension. Truly, the preachers of Heaven do not use words in vain, as sometimes we earthly ones do. With this small word, they give great instruction to those who are paying attention. Let us be among those who are paying attention!

He will so come in like manner as you saw Him go into Heaven. According to these words, which refer to the circumstances of Jesus Christ's Ascension into Heaven, first of all, we may note the blessing that He gave during the Ascension to the Apostles. As the Apostle Luke said, *Now it came to pass, while He blessed them, that He was parted from them and carried up into Heaven.* The Lord   Luke 24:51
Himself will remind His chosen of this specific detail concerning His Ascension and His being parted from them *when the Son of Man comes in His glory* to meet them once again, at which point   Matthew 25:31
He will call them to an active lordship over His Kingdom, for *then the King will say to those on His right hand, 'Come, you blessed of My Father, inherit the Kingdom prepared for you from the foundation of the world'.*   Matthew 25:34

What an endless pouring out of Christ's blessing reveals itself before us, O Christians! He begins the blessing, and, not having finished it, ascends. *Now it came to pass, while He blessed them...He was carried up into Heaven.* Having ascended in this way, He con-   Luke 24:51
tinues invisibly to give us His blessing. It pours forth and down onto the Apostles constantly; through them it passes to those whom they blessed in the name of Jesus Christ, and having received Christ's blessing through the Apostles, they spread that same blessing to others. Thus, everyone that belongs to the Holy,

Catholic, and Apostolic Church becomes a communicant of the single blessing of Jesus Christ and His Father, *who has blessed us with every spiritual blessing in the heavenly places in Christ*, like the dew of Hermon, *which falls upon the hills of Zion*. This blessing of the world descends to every soul that rises above passions and lusts, higher than the vanity and cares of this world, like a permanent impression that signals who is Christ's, so that at the end of this age, according to this sign, He will call them out from among the entire human race: *Come, you blessed of the Lord!*

<small>Ephesians 1:3</small>
<small>Psalm 132:3</small>
<small>Matthew 25:34</small>

Let us think, brothers, how we must labor to acquire and preserve the blessing of the ascended Lord that comes down on us through the Apostles and the apostolic Church. If we receive and preserve it, then together with the Apostles and all the Saints, we will be called, in the future coming of Jesus Christ, to participate in His Kingdom: *come, you blessed!* And if, at the time that He calls His chosen, we either do not have that blessing or we only possess the false blessing of people who themselves did not inherit the grace-filled and mysterious blessing of the heavenly Father, what will happen to us? Amen, I say unto you! Let us think of this and take care of it in time!

<small>Matthew 25:34</small>

Another aspect of the Ascension of the Lord that resonates with the Second Coming of the Lord is that the Lord ascended before the eyes of His disciples vividly and triumphantly. *While they watched, He was taken up, and a cloud received Him out of their sight*. What sort of a cloud was this? A cloud of light and glory that at one time shadowed and filled the tabernacle of Moses and the Temple of Solomon. There, the glory was evident, though not the Lord of glory; afterwards, He was evident, but not in His glory, and so they did not recognize Him and did not glorify Him. But here, neither does the glory hide the Glorified One, nor does the Glorified One hide His glory. The Apostles saw the glory of the ascended Lord. The Prophet heard it as well when he himself triumphantly exclaimed: *God is gone up with a merry noise, the Lord with the sound of the trumpet.*

<small>Acts 1:9</small>
<small>Psalm 46:6</small>

And so, when the light-bearing messengers told us that He would come in the same manner as they saw Him go into Heaven, they let us know that He would come both obviously and triumphantly. This is exactly what the Lord Himself said, that *the Son of Man comes in His glory, and all the holy Angels with Him.* Thus also the Apostle explains that *the Lord Himself will descend from Heaven with a shout, with the voice of an archangel, and with the trumpet of God.*

Matthew 25:31

1 Thessalonians 4:16

Some might ask why such details are noted, which seem less to provide instruction than to incite wonder, for prophecies are given for people to know and faithfully accept events that God sends; but the glorious Second Coming is known to all, even if not in specific details. Do not hurry, beloved brother, to make such conclusions about these details. No! The Apostles, the Angels, and the Lord Himself do not say anything to incite simple curiosity, but they always speak for instruction. That the coming of Christ will be evident and triumphant—this was foretold because there will be false Prophets giving contrary prophecies, when God will send a spirit of delusion on unworthy, unfaithful, and corrupt Christians. For a time of temptation will come, or perhaps it is already here, where they will say, *Look, [Christ] is in the desert!... or 'Look, He is in the inner rooms!' Do not believe it.*

Matthew 24: 23, 26

Here He is, with us! This is what such schismatics will say, who, having left the city of God, the spiritual Jerusalem, the apostolic Church, will not run to the true desert of peace and quiet, but into a wilderness of the spiritual and the sensual, where there is no true teaching or holiness of the mysteries, nor any good rule governing either private life or social life. Here He is, with us! This is what the heretics say quietly, pointing at their mysterious gatherings, as though the sun can only shine under the Earth, as though Christ had not said and commanded, *Whatever I tell you in the dark, speak in the light; and what you hear in the ear, preach on the housetops.*

Matthew 10:27

Hearing such words or such whisperings, remember, O Christians, the voice of the Angels and their prophecy concerning the ascended Lord: *He will so come in like manner as you saw Him go into Heaven*, just as evidently, just as triumphantly. And so, *If anyone says to you, 'Look, here is the Christ!' or 'There!' do not believe it.* Neither crude whining nor cunning whispering sound anything like the words of the archangel or the trumpet of God. *Do not go out* to follow those who call you out of the city of the Lord. Remain in your place and preserve your faith for the true coming of Christ, which will be glorious and triumphant. *(Acts 1:11; Matthew 24:23)*

The third aspect of the Ascension of the Lord that resonates with His future coming is that it was unexpected and surprising for His disciples. This occurred, as much as we can make out from the short Gospel accounts, in this way. He appeared to them in Jerusalem, as occurred often after His Resurrection, and then He led them out of the city, speaking with them, as usual, of the Kingdom of God, and especially concerning the imminent descent of the Holy Spirit: *And He led them out as far as Bethany, and He lifted up His hands and blessed them. Now it came to pass, while He blessed them, that He was parted from them and carried up into Heaven.* *(Luke 24:50-51)*

It was not only by His own will that He did not warn them about the great event of the coming of the Kingdom. He even refused firmly to answer their questions about it. *It is not for you to know times or seasons which the Father has put in His own authority.* This refusal to indicate times evidently referred also to His Second Coming, and in fact referred to that event in the first place. Even before, He had told His disciples of the suddenness of this event, comparing it to lightning that is the most vivid natural example of complete suddenness. *For as the lightning comes from the east and flashes to the west, so also will the coming of the Son of Man be.* Similarly, the Apostle Paul said, *The day of the Lord so comes as a thief in the night.* *(Acts 1:7; Matthew 24:27; 1 Thessalonians 5:2)*

About this suddenness of His future coming, the Lord Himself gives us, Christians, a salvific warning: *Watch therefore, for you do not known what hour your Lord is coming.* Do not become filled with curiosity or frivolity of faith when Christians, who think to know more than Christ Himself, begin to calculate the times of the His coming Kingdom and to indicate the exact year for His looked-for appearance: *It is not for you to know times or seasons which the Father has put in His own authority.* Strive instead to better know your own sins, to calculate your falls, and to find their limits in repentance. All the more be careful, if you hear the words of those fools prophesied by the Apostles: *Where is the promise of His coming? For since the fathers fell asleep, all things continue as they were from the beginning of creation.*

Matthew 24:42

Acts 1:7

2 Peter 3:4

Be careful, lest the dark delusions of the sons of this age, who shut their eyes against the light of the coming age, do not darken your hearts, do not blind your minds, do not put to sleep your spirits as they await that much desired and terrifying hour when the Lord will come *like a thief in the night.*

1 Thessalonians 5:2

Therefore, beloved, looking forward to these things, be diligent to be found by Him in peace, without spot and blameless. Amen!

2 Peter 3:14

22

Homily on Ascension (1825)

*Now when He had spoken these things,
while they watched, He was taken up,
and a cloud received Him out of their sight (Acts 1:9).*

The Lord ascended before the gaze of eleven Apostles. His Resurrection was without witnesses, but His Ascension had them. The glory of the Resurrection, in the moment of Resurrection, was hidden by the sealed stone tomb; a bright, transparent cloud revealed the glory of the Ascension when it occurred. Why this difference? Maybe for this reason. The Resurrection of the Lord, after His descent into Hell, was a movement from Hell to Paradise, and so there was nowhere to put the witnesses, and so the witnesses had to be those Patriarchs and Prophets who had departed this life. As for the Ascension, it was a movement from Earth to Heaven, and so it was natural for the Apostles to be witnesses, standing on Earth and looking up heavenward.

Moreover, it was sufficient to see the Resurrected One after the Resurrection—this was proof enough of the Resurrection. As for the Ascension of an earth-born body to Heaven, this needed to be seen in actual fact, in order to witness to it afterward. The carnal mindset immediately asks: can an earth-born body ascend to Heaven? We answer: there is no need to speculate on the possibility of this event when it was already seen and witnessed by people who were ready to die to prove the truth of what they witnessed.

However, did the Lord show His Ascension only for the sake of visible proof? Without a doubt, He did it also to give strength to the believers. *If then you were raised with Christ,* said the Apostle, and we add, if you saw Him ascend into Heaven and if you also desire to partake in this new triumph of His, *seek those things which are above, where Christ is, sitting at the right hand of God. Set your mind on things above, not on things on the Earth.* *Colossians 3:1-2*

What does it mean to set your mind on things above? Is it not true that this phrase is not very precise? However, if you don't understand, then, whether you like it or not, you have to admit that you are not yet doing this, that is, you have not yet set your mind on things above. After all, whoever acts already knows how to act. If you have not yet set your mind on things above, then you will not enter the higher places, *where Christ is, sitting at the right hand of God.* But if you do not go to that place where Christ is at the right hand of God, then think, you who are born on this Earth, what will happen to you when the visible Heaven and Earth pass away, and there will not be anything left outside the Heights of Paradise other than Hell? Look and see how the Earth is already crumbling beneath your feet, and Hell is opening up. There is no other means for salvation than to hold on with all your strength to the things which are above. We have to learn how to *seek those things which are above, not things on the Earth.* *Colossians 3:1-2*

How do we learn this? Let no one be afraid of this requirement. Let no one think that this requirement means being plunged into various difficulties that accompany what the world usually calls the acquisition of wisdom, and which includes the very methods of human wisdom — that is, a great number of teachers that all contradict one another, many books that often have deleterious effects both on the eyes (and not only from harmful dust!) and on the mind. Do not be afraid. To learn how to seek those things which are above is not the same as learning human wisdom. The wisdom from above is not so dependent on external circumstances, doesn't demand so many textbooks, isn't hindered by as many obstacles as earthly wisdom (even though it does use external circumstances), doesn't reject textbooks outright, and is not lacking in difficulties of a different nature.

The Apostle who wrote the command to seek the things which are above himself used the books and sources of earthly wisdom, having been raised at the feet of Gamaliel. But then, he rejected all this, as well as all other advantages of the flesh, as *rubbish* and *loss for the excellence of the knowledge of Christ Jesus my Lord... that I may gain Christ.* Consequently, he grew in knowledge of things above, in spite of the fact that at the same time he rejected the textbooks and sources of human wisdom. Other Apostles only knew how to weave fishing nets, not how to untangle the contradictions of human learning. But this did not prevent them, not only from succeeding in the knowledge of things above, but also from becoming instructors of this heavenly wisdom, even for the wise of this world.

Philippians 3:7-8

Thus, even after the apostolic age, St. Basil the Great acquired the wisdom of Athens, but considered it a slave to the knowledge of the Gospels. St. Arsenius, also called the Great, was great in the knowledge of the Greeks and Romans, but found himself to be still ignorant, while considering an illiterate Egyptian, his elder, to be knowledgeable enough to submit himself to his instruction in the beginnings of spiritual wisdom. And so, heavenly knowledge, though it is exalted even for wise men, remains simple enough for children. For *You have hidden these things from the wise and prudent and have revealed them to babes.*

Matthew 11:25

What does it mean to seek those things which are above? I repeat: if you don't understand, then evidently, you are not yet doing it. And if you do not seek these things, then there is no doubt that you seek the things of the Earth; consequently, you already know how to do that. And so, what do you do when you seek the things of this Earth, for example, when you think of how best to become rich? You desire the riches; often you think of them; you come up with ways to acquire and multiply them. You use the riches in action, not merely in thought. Whatever you do, you do it with the intention of acquiring and increasing your riches; you place all your happiness in the possession of these riches. According to this example, you can say in general that to seek the things of this Earth means to desire earthly things, to think of earthly things, to act in earthly ways, to have the earthly in your intentions, and to place your happiness in earthly things.

Change the object, and you will understand what it means to seek the things above. It means to desire the heavenly, or rather, the spiritual and the divine. It means to think of the heavenly, to act in heavenly ways, or, as the Gospel has it, to *work the works of God*. It means to have the heavenly as your object, and to place all your joy in the heavenly. *(John 6:28)*

How difficult, some may think. To have the heavenly in thought, in desire, in action — that means that an earthly person must change his deeds, his desires, and even his thoughts. I do not argue the point. This is indeed necessary, and it is not quite easy. But what is there to be done? To ascend a height is more difficult than to fall into a pit. Does that mean that is it better to fall into a pit?

It is difficult to seek the things above, but is it not also difficult to seek the things below? Is it easy, for example, for an avaricious man to seek earthly things? He works day and night; he deprives himself of food and rest. He sometimes leaves his home, leaving behind those dear to his heart. He traverses continents, sails the seas, descends into valleys, torturing himself either by the hunger for acquisition, or the care for maintenance, or the fear of possible loss, or the despair of losing everything. If he forces his thoughts to undergo such difficulties—and this only to be enriched with perishable treasures for a short time—then isn't it worth it to force the mind to acquire a heavenly treasure that does not perish for all time?

Yes, it is difficult for an earthly man to seek what is above; however, does not the seed of wheat, buried under your feet, seek what is above in its own way? It opens up; its shoot breaks through the soil, upward, fighting against the soil and its own weight. It grows higher and higher; and, striving constantly upward, it flowers and brings forth fruit. Do you really think that an earthly man has less strength than a plant to strive upward, as appropriate for his own kind?

It is difficult for an earthly man to seek the things above. However, are you completely earthly, O man? Is man nothing other than that part that is taken from Earth and returned to it? Is not this simply your clothing, or, if you like, your prison? While you, the true human being, you are the breath of life proceeding out of the mouth of God Himself, as it was written: "The Lord God formed man of the dust of the ground, and breathed into his nostrils the breath of life; and man became a living being" (Genesis 2:7). And so, if it is difficult for an earthly man, should it not be easy for you to set your mind on things above if you are a heavenly being? Is it difficult for fire to stream upward, where its natural place is? Is it difficult for a stone to fall to the earth from which it was born? Is it difficult for the spirit of man to strive upward, to approach the Most High?

If the fall of the old Adam transformed the striving of man from the things above to the things below and beneath the Earth, then does not the Resurrection and Ascension of the new Adam, the God-man, Jesus Christ, with even greater power turn man's striving back to its original direction? Did it not establish a ladder to the heavens? Did not the descent of the Holy Spirit light a spiritual fire in man spiritually, which naturally tends upward, pulling the vessel that it inhabits upward?

If it is difficult, even after this, to set your mind on things above, is it not at least worth it to change your deeds, your desires, and your thoughts, no matter what the difficulty?

But how can you abandon earthly deeds, desires, and thoughts when we are surrounded by the earthly, when the earthly is necessary for everyday life? If you pay attention to yourself and see how you abandon all that is heavenly for the sake of the earthly, you will find a very easy method for abandoning the earthly for the heavenly. You shorten the time you dedicate for deeds of piety to have more time for deeds of the world. Sometimes you go the temple of God, but you still think of everything that occupies you in your home. Sometimes, when you stand with your body in the temple of prayer, your thoughts go wherever the earthly mindset takes them, or the passions that lord them over you. Then, even your spiritual exercises are damaged by the earthly thoughts that come into their midst.

Act in the opposite way. Do the deeds that are necessary for earthly life. However, try not to stretch them out beyond what is necessary, and, as much as possible, free yourself from this work for the sake of the freedom of deeds of piety. Do not merely stand in God's presence in church, but prevent your thoughts from turning away to earthly things. But beyond this, when you are occupied with the necessary work of everyday life, distract your thoughts and desires from it, and instead raise them to the heavens and to God.

When you walk to your daily work, remember God, and ask His blessing and help. When you come back home to rest after work, remember God and thank Him for His help in this work and for the gift of rest. This is a way that you can train any worldly occupation, as long as it does not transgress God's law, to become united with a striving for things above. In this way, you can transform everything earthly and visible into spiritual and heavenly realities.

As St. Makarius the Great said, "If you look at the sun, seek the true sun, for you are blind. When you pass your gaze over the light, turn your eyes inward to your soul, and see whether or not it contains the true and good light, that is, the Lord Himself."

May the light of our Lord, Jesus Christ, enlighten you, may His Spirit strengthen you, may your striving after His words and life raise every one of us to a striving for things above, and through this, to the blessed vision of God in His heavens, where Christ Himself sits at the right hand of God. Amen.

23

Homily on the Ascension and the uncovering of the Relics of St. Alexis (1854)

No living person saw the Resurrection of Christ at the exact mysterious moment that it happened. Perhaps it was impossible for physical eyes to see Christ's visible body transfiguring into a spiritual one as He stepped outside the boundaries of the visible world. Moreover, it was probably intended this way because faith had not yet come to grips with such a mystical vision. For a heavenly and divine apparition is enlightening and life-giving only for those who are prepared for it through faith, purity, love of God, and humility. For those who are unprepared and impure, it is like being struck by lightning. Most likely, God wanted to make room for a deed of faith, so that we could receive its great reward. *Blessed are they that have not seen, and yet have believed.* John 20:29

Conversely, many people did witness the Ascension of the Lord with their own eyes. Of course, this was because the faith of many had become prepared for such a divine sight.

The holy Evangelist Luke bears witness to the fact that it was not only the Eleven Apostles, but many others who saw the Lord ascend. If the Lord Himself wanted the sight of His Ascension to be so accessible, then let us follow the words of this eyewitness. Perhaps, we will better understand how the Angels themselves looked at the Ascension with the same wonder as we. May the Gospel of our holy Evangelist Luke be our guide.

Luke 24:33

He writes, *He led them out as far as to Bethany.* During the forty days that the resurrected Lord appeared to the Apostles, *[He spoke] of the things pertaining to the Kingdom of God.* On the fortieth day, He appeared to them in Jerusalem. Walking before them, He guided them through the streets of the city and walked out of it through the gate leading to the Mount of Olives.

Luke 24:50

Acts 1:3

What about Jerusalem? Did it see the crucified and resurrected One, but failed to believe its own eyes out of bitterness? Or did it see Him, but did not recognize Him because of its faithlessness, as happened for a short time with the two disciples on the road to Emmaus? Or did the blindness of their lack of faith prevent them from seeing Him at all, though the faithful at the very same time could see, hear, and feel Him? Whichever way it was, what a terrible blindness! What a miserable fate! Christ does not yet appear before the Christ-killing city as a Judge, but as a Savior. He is ready to listen to repentance and to show mercy, but the self-condemned city "knew not the time of [His] visitation" (Luke 19:44). The Savior walked through its streets and left its gates to clearly fulfill that which He had spoken before, *Behold, your house is left to you desolate.*

Matthew 23:38

Brethren! Let us beware such lack of faith! Beware this inattention to grace-filled, divine visitations, for it could result in disastrous blindness. Some might say, "Why all these suspicions and fears?" "Are we Jews?" "What grace-filled miracles did we miss through our inattention?"

This is true, we are not the Jews of the Old Testament. By God's grace, we are the new Israel. However, we know that God chose Israel of old for its faith and grace. For its faithlessness after faith, for its sin after the Law, God punished it for the sake of correction many times. And finally, since it refused correction, God cast Israel away.

But why do you think that something similar cannot happen to the new Israel? Grace-filled visitations are not as rare as you think. When you hear the Gospel in church, does Christ not come and stand before you? Does He not speak with you? Does He not work miracles before you? And still, after all this, some people leave the church as though they did not see or hear any of it, continuing to wallow in their passions and sensual desires, as though Christ, His teachings, and His example pertain to some other world. Don't these people resemble the inhabitants of Jerusalem, who walked past Christ without recognizing Him, *leaving their house desolate?* *Matthew 23:38*

Who knows how long He, by His mercy, will want to *gather [us]...as a hen gathers her chickens under her wings*, if we are inattentive and disobedient to His grace? Perhaps He will once again speak His word of judgment, but this time to us: *Behold, your house is left unto you desolate.* Let us return to the Gospel and follow it further. *And He led them out as far as to Bethany, and He lifted up his hands, and blessed them.* The resurrected Lord did not only appear to His disciples in Jerusalem. He also appeared to them on the road to Emmaus, in Galilee, and on the banks of the Sea of Galilee. Why then did He not simply appear to them at the place He had chosen for His Ascension? Why did He appear to them in Jerusalem, then lead them out of it? *Matthew 23:37* *Matthew 23:38* *Luke 24:50*

There is no doubt that this action, like all the actions of divine wisdom, had a deeper meaning. It meant that Christ's grace had departed from ancient Jerusalem that *received him not*. Jerusalem willingly assumed the guilt of His Blood, spilled for the salvation of the world. Through this faithlessness and deicide, Jerusalem prepared its own abandonment and destruction. He had not come to destroy the souls of men, but to save those who were surrounded by ruin, and so, He began to choose those who could be saved. *John 1:11*

He took the best stones out of the ancient city, and with the artistry of a heavenly Architect, He prepared them for a new building with words of righteousness and salvation. He did this to show that He came not to serve the old and obsolete, not to put a new patch on old garments, not to pour new wine into old wineskins, but to make new vestments of salvation, new vessels of grace, a new living city of the Kingdom of Heaven on Earth. He carried His chosen living stones out of the ancient city to a free, pure, and high place.

Here, He blessed His newly created Church, much like He blessed His new heavenly creation. "And He led them out as far as Bethany, and He lifted up His hands, and blessed them." He lifted up His hands to Heaven and stretched them over those He blessed. He did this as a sign that He gave them a heavenly blessing which would reach all the way to *the deep places of the Earth*.

Psalm 95:4

What words did He use to bless them? St. Luke does not say; however, we believe that these words were such a stream of divine grace, power, and life, that it not only filled the vessels who were present there, but also stretched out to the whole of the Church of Christ, even to the very last true Christian before the Second Coming. It is likely that Christ's words were given to us by St. Matthew: *I am with you always, even unto the end of the world.*

Matthew 28:20

And it came to pass, while He blessed them, He was parted from them, and was carried up into Heaven. Notice that the Evangelist does not say "after He blessed" but *while He blessed*, meaning that His blessing does not end. What a wonderful action! The Lord blesses us and continues to do so, even as He ascends to Heaven. What does this mean? It means the He does not want to end His blessing, but rather continue to endlessly bless His Church and all those who believe in Him.

Luke 24:51
Luke 24:51

Imagine, brethren, if we believe, then we are also under His outstretched hands, His gaze, and His blessing. What joy for those who love Him! What shame and fear for those, who in the vanity of the world, forget Him!

The place where the Ascension of the Lord occurred is the Mount of Olives. Why was it chosen for this event? Why not some other place? Perhaps because He had visited it before, sanctifying it with many visits and prayers. After all, this was the place where He began His sufferings, His sorrows that were as heavy as death, and His prayer that was so painful that He sweated blood. By turning the place in which His sufferings began into the place of His glorification, He showed that His suffering and glorification comprised the same building block of God's salvific plan. They are both links in a single golden chain forged in the crucible of God's wisdom, for the return of fallen man to the heavens.

Christians! If fate brings you dark and troubling news, do not fall prey to sorrow or anguish, but rather see these things as a sign of Christ's path. If He who was innocent deigned to suffer the sorrows and anguish of death for our sins, will you not submit to carry an undoubtedly smaller burden of sorrow? Perhaps you are innocent before men, but surely you have sinned before God! Follow Christ, even if from afar, and utter a powerful, God-inspired prayer. Then, have hope that your salvation will come soon after your sorrows if you hold to Christ's path — the path of purity and devoted patience to God. *He that shall endure unto the end, the same shall be saved.* *Mark 13:13*

What is the limit of the Lord's Ascension? If it is possible to answer such a question, then we will find the answer in the words of the Apostle: *He that descended is the same also that ascended up far above all heavens, that he might fill all things.* Let us add that the ascended Lord *sat on the right hand of God.* *Ephesians 4:10* *Mark 16:19*

After hearing this, the listener should not imagine anything earthly or sensual. When you hear a person call another person, "my right hand," of course you do not think that that person has turned into a hand! It describes intimacy between friends. Ideally, such a friend complements you in the same way that a right hand complements the left.

Furthermore, you should avoid physical categories when describing the spiritual; otherwise, would you not limit the eternal to a single location? When you read that Christ *sat on the right hand of God*, interpret that to mean that He and the Father have a single, united power, glory, and will in their governance of the whole world, especially the Church of those being saved. In general, you should limit your thoughts from flying too high to the boundless heights where *the light which no man can approach* dwells.

_{Mark 16:19}

_{1 Timothy 6:16}

If your eye is powerless before the light of the sun, then how much more shall the eye of your impure mind become powerless before the light of the eternal Sun of souls. Before Him, even the highest Angels hide their faces. Even the Apostles' gazes could not follow the ascending Lord, for a cloud covered Him and hid Him from them. And just as they fell down and *worshipped Him*, so must you. After you gaze humbly with faith to the heavens, then you should fall in humility, you son of dust, to the dust. Honor the unspeakable Majesty with silent reverence.

_{Luke 24:52}

The effect that the Lord's Ascension had on the Apostles may seem unexpected: *And they returned to Jerusalem with great joy.* One might think that they would be saddened by being separated from their divine Teacher and Savior, yet they were very joyful. Why is this? They rejoiced because their faith was fulfilled and their mind was opened to comprehend the mysteries of Christ. They believed and knew that with His Resurrection, Christ destroyed the gates of Hell and let the faithful out of it. Through His Ascension, He opened the doors to Heaven, leading all faithful inside those doors.

_{Luke 24:52}

They rejoiced because their love was fulfilled. It was sweet for them that their beloved Savior ascended to the heavens in bliss and glory, though they remained on Earth to labor and suffer. They rejoiced because their hope was fulfilled. They knew and anticipated that the ascended Lord, as He promised, would quickly send them a Comforter, the Holy Spirit. And finally, according to the prophecy of the Angel, "*Jesus, who is taken up from you into Heaven, shall so come in like manner.* They now knew, without a doubt, that He would come to fulfill His other promise: *I will come again, and receive you unto Myself.*

Acts 1:11

John 14:3

Brethren, if we wish to share the joy of the Apostles, then know this: it is ours to partake in also. Listen to what the Apostle Peter says about those who are faithful to and love Christ: *Whom having not seen, you love; in whom, though now you see Him not, yet believing, you rejoice with joy unspeakable and full of glory.* Therefore, guard your living faith in Christ, arouse your love for Him, and remain steadfast in your hope in Him. If you remain faithful, you will *rejoice with joy unspeakable and full of glory*. Finally, let us emulate the way the Apostles preserved and nourished the grace given to them at the Ascension of the Lord. They *were continually in the temple, praising and blessing God.*

1 Peter 1:8

1 Peter 1:8

Luke 24:53

Heirs of Heaven! Why do our thoughts and desires roam all over the Earth? Let us gather them before the threshold of Heaven. Let us be continually at the Temple, inseparably united with it in faith, in diligent communion with her prayers and mysteries, in active obedience to her rules and teachings. This is our path to Heaven; there is no other.

Teach us *Your way, O Lord* and let us *walk in Your truth*. Lead us through the prayers of our immortal pastor, St. Alexis. Amen.

Psalm 86:11

24

Homily on Pentecost (1811)

And they were all filled with the Holy Spirit (Acts 2:4).

Genesis 3:8

After he had plunged into the depths of materialism, no longer being able to bear the uncreated light, man *hid* from God, and God hid from man (lest God destroy him by His holy presence). Then, the one God in three Persons, in His inexpressible goodness, once again approached man's estrangement in gradual revelations, so that *the grace of the Lord Jesus Christ, and the love of God, and the communion of the Holy Spirit* would once again raise up and exalt fallen man.

2 Corinthians 13:14

The Father revealed Himself in His promises of love and mercy and He led the sinner, who was terrified by the all-powerful justice of God, to the mediation of the Son. The Son appeared in the form of man, and the Son having defeated sin in Himself and having trampled down death, opened the door for the grace of the Holy Spirit to enter the sons of wrath. Finally, the Holy Spirit Himself appeared in the sign of the fiery tongues and entered deep into the Apostles' human nature, so that they would be able to acquire the good will of the Father, the merits of the Son, and become *partakers of the divine essence*. *2 Peter 1:4*

On the same day as the Law of the spirit of "bondage and fear" was given on Sinai, the Law of *the Spirit of life, freedom, and adoption* flowed forth from Zion. Therefore, let us understand what earthly Israel did not understand—the justification of the Law is fulfilled in the children of faith who walk in the Spirit. The community of those being saved move by preordained steps toward perfection. *Romans 8:15, 2*

Thus, we must look at the descent of the Holy Spirit, not only as a miracle that glorified the apostolic Church, but also as an event that is essentially connected with the work of our own salvation. Today's triumph is not only a simple remembrance of what occurred, but also a continuation of the apostolic preparation for the acceptance of this Spirit who *blows where [He] wishes*. The Apostles, as the Book of Acts tells us, after constant prayers in common, *were all filled with the Holy Spirit* and this was true not only of the Apostles, but, according to the explanation of St. Chrysostom, it also included the disciples with them, *[whose] number of names was about a hundred and twenty*. And today the Church, as in the upper room on Zion, unites us all together to invoke the Comforter, the Spirit of truth, that He would come down and abide in us. *John 3:8*
Acts 2:4
Acts 1:15

Lest such an important invocation be met with the ancient rebuke: *You do not know what you ask*, let us try to understand, dear listeners, what it means to be filled with the Holy Spirit. Let us try to understand how necessary this gift is for every one of us. *Matthew 20:22*

We do not dare to speak here of the Holy Spirit in His essence, who is the third Person of the worshipful Trinity, who proceeds from the Father and abides in the Son, *the Spirit [who] searches... the deep things of God*. However, regarding the Spirit as sent by the Son from the Father through His salvific gifts, the Spirit who fills man, and the man who is filled with the Spirit—these are subjects that man, illumined by the same Spirit, can understand. *1 Corinthians 2:10*
John 15:26

We, who barely have *the first fruits of the Spirit*, can only plumb the depth of this great mystery from a distance, through the mirror of the word of God.

Who is the Holy Spirit in His initial gifts? He Himself explains this by His fiery tongues. He is the immaterial fire that acts through two powers——light and warmth, specifically, the light of faith and the warmth of love. This heavenly light, according to Solomon's expression, *shines ever brighter unto the perfect day*. It dispels the darkness of unbelief and doubt. It reveals the delusion of phantoms that the mind, plunged deep in a carnal mindset, often assumes to be the truth. It allows man to see himself in the nakedness of his corrupted nature, to know the world with the soul and to feel the presence of God as the source of that heavenly light. It gives *the substance of things hoped for, the evidence of things not seen*. The more the light from the Sun of Righteousness increases in the mind, the more the heart becomes warm and catches spiritual fire.

Divine love banishes self-love; it burns away the thorns of carnal desires and purifies the heart. At the same time, it also attracts a new light into the soul. The combination of these gifts of the Spirit creates a fiery tongue that, uttering the Law of God the Word in the heart of man, in whom *Christ is formed*, perfects our rebirth into spiritual life.

The way a person is filled with spiritual gifts is by the single, undivided action of the Holy Spirit. However, in man, this action begins and ends, lessens and grows, delays and hurries, and takes various forms and directions. It always depends on the readiness of the recipient, but it never depends on his will. It is accompanied by tangible signs, but it rushes away from rationalizations that seek to explain away its source. Flowing from the internal to the external, it is similar to the dew that came down on the fleece of Gideon, which came from the air and revealed itself in drops of water that filled a vessel. Or rather, it is

Romans 8:23

Proverbs 4:18

Hebrews 11:1

Galatians 4:19

Judges 4:38

like a wind that is only visible in the movement that it produces in external objects.

The wind blows where it wishes, and you hear the sound of it, but cannot tell where it comes from and where it goes. So is everyone who is born of the Spirit. What are the observable changes that can indicate the coming of the Spirit of God into the soul of a person? There are moments during which even a man dedicated to the world and the flesh awakens from his entranced state. He sees clearly that his past life is a chain of delusions, weaknesses, sins, and betrayals of God. His actions are the natural seeds of future punishments and even his virtues will not stand before the gaze of the eternal Judge. He condemns himself, trembling with his entire essence, and being completely in despair of himself, but yet through this despair, he is led to hope in God. This disposition toward repentance is nothing other than the same *great and strong [Spirit that] tore into the mountains and broke the rocks in pieces,* that threw down pride and softened hard hearts—the Spirit that the Lord, who "passed by", sent before His face. What is this disposition but the same fear of the Lord, through which we *have been with child, we have been in pain; we have, as it were, brought forth [the Spirit]?* *John 3:8*

3 Kingdoms 19:11

Isaiah 26:18

Blessed is he who humbly submits to this movement of the Spirit of God! For the Spirit will lead him by the *narrow path* of self-rejection. The Spirit will force him to throw away what he sowed before, to destroy what he built. The Spirit will teach him to suffer and rejoice in his sufferings, to *crucify the flesh with its passions and lusts,* so that his spirit will completely submit to the hand of God. *Matthew 7:14*

Colossians 1:23
Galatians 5:24

Little by little, the stormy winds will transform to calm *groanings which cannot be uttered,* by which *the Spirit Himself makes intercession*; they will transform into that living voice in *your hearts, crying out, Abba Father!* Then, man will fulfill Christ's commandment to pray without ceasing, which would be impossible with man's own strength because of his tendency to be distracted and

Romans 8:26
Galatians 4:6
Luke 18:1

his lack of knowledge about true prayer, *for we do not know what we should pray for as we ought.*

_{Romans 8:26}

Through this practice of constant prayer, spiritual solitude becomes habitual in which the Christian, *when he prays, goes into his room, and [shuts] the door.* The Christian then abides, like the Apostles, in the expectation of the *promise of the Father.* Such a person does not fall into distraction, because of which the lovers of the world, tied by vain decorum, seeking vain comforts, and persecuted by cares, rarely turn inward. No, the true Christian brings *every thought into captivity to the obedience of Christ* and either raises all his desires on high, where his *life is hidden with Christ in God,* or else he hides them inside himself, where grace, finally, must reveal the Kingdom of God.

_{Matthew 6:6}
_{Acts 1:4}

_{2 Corinthians 10:5}

_{Colossians 3:3}
_{Luke 17:21}

The true Christian fulfills the responsibilities of his earthly profession without becoming attached to any benefits he receives from it. He uses earthly benefits, but he doesn't attach himself to them. He acquires objects as though he had no need of them, and he loses them as though he were just giving away the excess. If a man firmly decides, as much as is possible, to keep himself in this state of self-rejection then very soon his *desert shall rejoice and blossom as the rose, like a mustard seed, which a man took and put in his garden; and it grew and became a large tree.* Through the *old man with his deeds,* from hour to hour, *you [will] put on the new man which was created according to God, in true righteousness and holiness,* and the Spirit of holiness will breathe through all the new man's talents and actions.

_{Isaiah 35:1}
_{Luke 13:19}
_{Colossians 3:8}
_{Ephesians 4:24}

To the eye that is not darkened by prejudice, such a person, filled with the Holy Spirit, appears to be such an image of perfection that everything that the world calls wonderful or exalted disappears before him as shadows before light. Dear listeners, this is what the Apostle meant when speaking of certain zealots of the faith: they are those *of whom the world was not worthy.* Grace transforms everything that it touches in man into a priceless

_{Hebrews 11:38}

treasure. From his mind shines forth the spirit of wisdom——not the wisdom that the sons of this age prioritize, according to the Lord's words, *in their generation*; not the wisdom that teaches us to be resourceful in means and brave in circumstances that call for the acquisition of temporary benefits; but the kind of wisdom that increases our dignity, not so much within ourselves, as in the opinion of others.

Luke 16:8

No, here I speak of the wisdom that *spiritually judges all things*, so that everything can become a means to the single, eternal benefit of the soul. The Spirit of freedom drives the spiritual man's will, for *the law of the Spirit of the life in Christ Jesus has made me free from the law of sin and death* that burdens its slaves with so many cruel masters, so many needs and desires, and passions and habits. In the depth of such a man's heart, there abides a spirit of comfort and peace that *surpasses all understanding*, which Jesus Christ gives His disciples, *not as the world gives*.

2 Corinthians 2:15

Romans 8:2

Philippians 4:7
John 14:27

For the peace of the world is a short nap during a terrible storm, a safety founded on ignorance, so that the joyful exclamation, "Peace and safety!", is sometimes interrupted by *sudden destruction [that] comes upon them*. On the contrary, the peace of Christ is founded on unbreakable certitude in one's reconciliation with God so that the Christian, even in the midst of temptations, sorrows, and dangers, is *not in despair*, but is even *delivered to death* calmly, knowing that *our light affliction, which is but for a moment, is working for us a far more exceeding and eternal weight of glory*.

1 Thessalonians 5:3

2 Corinthians 4:8-17

In such a transformed person the spirit of greatness abides, which is neither blind bluster, nor puffed-up pride, nor the glister of natural virtues that are impure in their source; , but rather a true exaltedness of thoughts that are busy with a contemplation of God, a vista of views limited only by eternity, a nobility of emotions that are born and cultivated by the word of God—a spirit of humility that even in the midst of the riches of the berefits of God sees only its own poverty and unworthiness, all the more to glorify the Lord.

However, the person who is not reborn by the Spirit of God tries to find something exalted in his own limitations. He asks for respect based on his own humiliation, and he slithers on the ground to smother others. The power of such an unregenerated spirit makes a Christian as powerless as all others, a slave of his own emotions, surrounded on all sides by the attacks of enemies, defeated even before the battle begins; indeed, constantly being defeated by one passion, even if only to calm down another passion.

Not so the brave warrior, who *puts on the whole armor of God*, who *can do all things through Christ who strengthens* him, and who *takes [Heaven] by force!* What shall we say of the wondrous "diversities of gifts and manifestations of the Spirit" that those chosen by God receive for *the profit of all*, for the establishment of the entire Church?

Ephesians 6:11
Philippians 4:13
Matthew 11:12

1 Corinthians 12:4,7

O how unutterably glorious it is to be the vessel, the dwelling place, the tool of the Spirit of God! O what heavenly blessedness on Earth! O what a mystery, which contains everything hidden that the spirit of man seeks and everything for which *creation groans and labors with birth pangs ... until now!* However, *Who has believed our report? And to whom has the arm of the Lord been revealed? Flesh and blood have not revealed this* mystery. The world thinks that even those in Heaven breathe the air of this world, and no matter how many times it hears those who speak with the tongue of Your Spirit, O God, it continues to mock, as before: *They are full of new wine.*

Romans 8:22
Isaiah 53:1
Matthew 16:17

Acts 2:13

And so there are, even among us Christians, people who consider the gifts of the Holy Spirit so strange that if they do not completely reject them, at the very least they ascribe them only to other people and other ages. They themselves, thinking nothing of rebirth, are content to remain either in a vain hope in the merits of the Intercessor, or even in their own honor.

Let us not fool ourselves with the attractive external appearance of typical earthly honor. To not be an enemy of the faith, to not perform egregious acts of unfairness, to occasionally give alms, and to avoid harmful excesses—in short, to only do the absolutely necessary and external responsibilities demanded of a human being as a member of society—this is nothing but whitewashing your own tomb, which all the while remains *full of dead men's bones and all uncleanness*. Such a life is nothing other than tearing off the branches of the tree of life, given *for the healing of the nations*, but never eating the fruits that give life. Such a life is filled with the righteousness of the scribes and Pharisees, which does not lead to the Kingdom of Heaven. *Matthew 23:27* *Revelation 22:2* *Matthew 5:20*

Instead, plunge deep into the dark recesses of your own heart, from which *proceed evil thoughts, murders, adulteries, fornications, thefts, false witness, and blasphemies*, and there strive to enthrone purity and holiness, to *keep the whole law*, not being guilty even in *one point*, lest you be *guilty of all*. How can any man left only to his own wits and strength ever claim that he can accomplish all this? God alone creates *a clean heart and renew[s] a right spirit* in man. Man must be born from above to see the Kingdom of God. *Matthew 15:19* *James 2:10* *Psalm 50:12* *John 3:3*

On the other hand, even though the *incorruptible seed* of this rebirth from above came down to Earth through the death of the God-man, we still cannot ascribe all the rest to the power of His merits alone, though they be endless! How is this true? Has God condemned His own Son to be a victim not only to His own Justice, but to our own ingratitude? Have we come to know the actuality of the sacrifice of the Cross only to remain with even greater carelessness in our own lack of action? To think thus would not be to exalt the power of Christ's merits, but rather to denigrate them and trust in them with the same dangerous trust as the Jews once placed on the Law of Moses. If we have been baptized into Christ, then, according to this confession, we must reveal within ourselves the fruits of this baptism not only *1 Peter 1:23* by water but by spirit; for Christ *baptize[s] with the Holy Spirit and fire.* [Matthew 3:11]

Finally, though the divine gift of the Spirit seems to us a rare manifestation, we should not assume that this gift is not for all people. It is indeed for all, or rather, all are for it. If we no longer notice its manifestations, then either we have eyes that do not see, or perhaps the time has come of which Christ asked, *when the Son of Man comes, will He really find faith on the Earth?* [Luke 18:8] If that be the case, then the world itself is breathing its last. The cosmos knows what happened to it when an angered God said, *My Spirit shall not strive with man forever, for he is indeed flesh.* [Genesis 6:3] Therefore, it was not only the lawless race of man, but also creation (which had unwillingly become subject to vanity), that was buffeted by angry waves. There is yet another possible punishment: the fiery deluge of the final judgment will come!

But while God preserves our existence, O Christians, and upholds the prosperity of His Church, we must not doubt that the Spirit of God abides in it. Just as during the creation of the world, *the Spirit of God [hovers] over the face of the waters*, [Genesis 1:2] thus He also hovers today during the continuing re-creation of mankind, over the abyss of our corrupted nature. And by His live-giving visitation, He gives fruit to mankind to help this grace-filled re-birth. Let us give ourselves up to His all-powerful action. Let us lead our thoughts and desires to Him from the pollution of the flesh and the world. Let us call out from the depths of our fallenness, that He would come down on us by His grace, through the intercession of our Redeemer. And then, purify, enlighten, renew, sanctify, and save our souls, O Good One. Amen.

25

Homily on Pentecost (1814)

Be filled with the Spirit (Ephesians 5:18).

The soul of any feast day is the presence of the One being celebrated. And for those who celebrate the day of the Holy Spirit, what could be more desirable than for this heavenly Comforter to visit His own feast day through His grace? If He will not come down on us with tongues of fire, may He at least touch our hearts with a spark of His fire and light them aflame with the sense of God's presence, as He did once to the hardened hearts of the two disciples whose hearts hinted to them at least the vestige of the presence of the Lord: *Did not our hearts burn within us while He talked with us on the road, and while He opened the Scriptures to us?* *Luke 24:32*

This gift is so great that I do not know if we can ask it from the "Treasury of good things" without internal trepidation and a certain level of wonder at our own brazenness. Even so, the Church, every day and at the beginning of each time of prayer, invites us to invoke the Holy Spirit in these words, not only that He "come" to us, but that He "abide in us."

However, that which is so difficult for us to grasp even as a desire, the Holy Spirit Himself offers to us as reality, so simply and so graciously by the words of the Apostle; and not only does He offer it, but He commands, inspires, and enshrines it as law: *Be filled with the Spirit!* [Ephesians 5:18]

What a blessed, and yet what a wondrous and unattainable command do you give us, O divine Paul! *Be filled with the Spirit*—is it in our power to be filled with the Spirit? If this treasure is so close and so attainable, then why is it so rare and unknown?

O Christians! Of course, among our Ephesian fellow-Christians, to whom the teacher of the Gentiles first gave the command that we examine here, there was not a single person who would not have understood him in this case, and who might have offered him our own confusion. Otherwise, the divinely inspired teacher, without a doubt, would have said something to warn off doubts. Therefore, "those who thirsted" knew, during that time, of the path indicated by the Prophet Isaiah that they should *come to the waters; and you who have no money, come, buy, and eat. Yes, come, buy wine and milk without money and without price.* [Isaiah 55:1] It seems to us that the Lord considered the worth of His benefits too highly, as though it is not our muscles that have become weak, but His hand that has gotten shorter in the giving of spiritual gifts.

No! The Lord *pour[s] [His] Spirit on all flesh.* [Joel 2:28] If we will not be filled with the Spirit, it's not that there will not be enough of His gifts for us, rather, it is that we will not be enough for His gifts. May those who are poor in spirit be comforted! May those who are weak in flesh be raised up! May the Lord be justified in His words!

There was a time when the Apostles, who were first and foremost temples of the Holy Spirit, did not feel Him living in them. They already had the power to perform miracles, but they did not yet understand the source and did not recognize the direction of the power that acted within them. The Spirit of love appeared inside them as the spirit of anger, and those who were called to the service of salvation were ready to call down a consuming fire from Heaven! Then, Truth Himself rebuked them in such a strange ignorance of their own selves: *You do not know what manner of spirit you are of.* *Luke 9:55*

Afterward, when the same Spirit, (who had initially acted in the Apostles through a hidden power), visited them with His triumphant descent, He filled them with knowledge and wisdom. They came to know Him so clearly and so intimately that they could distinguish between Him and their own spirit, as well as that common spirit that acts in natural humanity and which had not yet been reborn by the Spirit of God, perhaps never even having felt His activity at all. As for us, says one of them, *now we have received, not the spirit of the world, but the Spirit who is from God, that we might know the things that have been freely given to us by God.* *1 Corinthians 2:12*

Let us note, dear listeners, that the Apostle didn't say that the Spirit was given to us, but that we received Him. It is as though he is clearly saying that God gives His Spirit to everyone who is ready to accept Him. Except, most people are burdened and darkened by the spirit of the world. We, however, have rejected the mastery of this dark spirit, and have instead accepted our spirit to be the light-bearing influence of the Spirit who proceeds from God; and thus, the active knowledge and sensation of the gifts of God has revealed itself in us. *Now we have received, not the spirit of the world, but the Spirit who is from God, that we might know the things that have been freely given to us by God.* *1 Corinthians 2:12*

And so, do not believe us, the weak servants of the word, but believe those chosen tools, messengers, and evangelists of the Spirit of God; that in spite of the somewhat independent existence and freedom of mankind, man can not only find himself, but often does indeed find himself under the rule of one of two principles, either the "spirit of this world" or "the Spirit who is from God," depending on which activity he freely chooses himself. If you do not yet sense this in your own lives, that only means that *You do not know what manner of spirit you are of.* *Luke 9:55*

To at least approach, as much as possible, the knowledge of these mysteries of the relationship between the spirit of man and the Spirit of God, we are allowed to use parables and guesses, into which divine truth clothed itself, to better appear before the gaze of men who are more or less sensual. A child in the womb has its own soul and life, but its life is submerged in the life of its mother, filled with it, fed by it, so that in comparison with the full life of a human being after birth, it can hardly be called life at all. This is a metaphor for that state in which natural man exists in the world.

The natural man's spirit has its own life and freedom, but all the same, being embodied, he is enveloped and imperceptibly ruled by the powers of this world. He thinks, but by the elements of this world. He desires, but only as ruled by the desires of the flesh, the desire of the eyes, and the pride of life, all of which rule over this world. He acts, but only in a small and narrow circle of the sensual. He lives, but by the spirit of the world, *being alienated from the life of God*.

Ephesians 4:18

It should be said that the seclusion of the child in the womb is not the intention of nature, only a means and a path by which the child is led to full life. It must come out into the light, see the beauty of the world, taste of its goodness, come to know its Creator--this is the highest calling of the human spirit, which is enveloped in the flesh and imprisoned in the world. *You must be born again*, for this, in God's intention, is not some chance fate for some people, but an enshrined law and the foreordained fate of all mankind, toward which all of natural life is nothing but a preparation and a passageway.

John 3:7

The prisoner of the world must be led out of his prison, to confess the name of the Lord, to be enlightened by the light of Christ, *to taste the heavenly gift, and...the powers of the age to come*, even during this age, to accept, even in this life, the Spirit which is from God, to begin on Earth to breathe the air of Heaven. As a child is born, as he is cut off from the life of the mother, he has no difficulty in finding his own new life, for the child carries

Psalm 141:8
Hebrews 6:4-5

within himself the source of activity that is constantly developing and being perfected, and so it finds the necessary air for life all around him. In the same way, led by grace from the world and called to a higher birth, man is already closer to the region of the new life than he realizes, for only we can be far from the Spirit of God, not He from us. This Spirit, according to the words of the Preacher, *goes through all understanding, pure, and most subtle spirits*, being untouchable in His holiness and everywhere present in His goodness. He pours forth on all powers and abilities that are given to His purview, and in the very heart of the old man, He opens up a source of new life. *He who believes in Me*, said the Giver of the Spirit, *out of his heart will flow rivers of living water... But this*, adds the beloved Disciple, *He spoke concerning the Spirit, whom those believing in Him would receive.* Wis. of Solomon 7:23

John 7:38-39

Finally, here is the important difference between natural and spiritual birth. The first is achieved by the necessary movement of nature, while the second is achieved through the free striving toward God made by faith in Christ. *He who believes in me, as the Scripture has said, out of his heart will flow rivers of living water.* And why entire rivers from a single womb, when a single drop from His grace is enough to give life to hosts of spirits? In order, as the Scripture has said, to reveal the extraordinary riches of His goodness, according to which the Holy Spirit not only fills, but overfills the measure of our readiness to accept Him. In other words, He gives us more than we accept. John 7:38

O Children of faith, is it right for us to not recognize the presence of the Holy Spirit among us and to ask of His dominion: where is He? Even before His triumphant descent to the Kingdom of faith, the children of the Law felt His omnipresent and omnipotent power so vividly that nowhere could they hide from it or rest from their reverent awe! *Where can I go from Your Spirit? Or where can I flee from Your presence?* This is what David exclaimed. And so, should we then be disturbed at how the independent human spirit can possibly stand under the constant action of the all-powerful Spirit? Even during the time of Job, people knew Psalm 138:7

that *there is a spirit in man, and the breath of the Almighty gives him understanding*. Should we also remember our own confession, so often renewed by the voice of the Church, by which, when we lead ourselves to prayerful closeness with God, we announce the omnipresent and all-fulfilling power of His Spirit? "Everywhere present and filling all things!"

"Filling all things!" But why are not all we also filled with Him? Evidently, we must ask ourselves that question.

Can we be filled with the Spirit if the flesh, constantly battling with the spirit, finds within us no barrier to its own dominion? What if in our rush for satiety, fullness, and pleasure, we shut out our spirit's thirst to hear the word of God and our hunger for the truth, which is so natural to our spirit? What if we only live for this flesh, in which, as the man of God assures us from his own experience, *nothing good dwells*? In this case, we subject ourselves to the heavy judgment of God, uttered over the first-created world: *My Spirit shall not strive with man forever, for he is indeed flesh. Whatever a man sows, that he will also reap. For he who sows to his flesh will of the flesh reap corruption, but he who sows to the Spirit will of the spirit reap everlasting life.*

Can we be filled with the Spirit of God if we only inspire ourselves with the spirit of this world? If we only fill our minds with its stormy wisdom, only enliven our imagination with the world's attractions, only excite our hearts with the world's passions, only direct our will by its laws, and try to oblige only the world with our actions? If our best emotions and even our virtues are infected with the corrupting inspiration of the spirit of this world—our love with obsessions, our condescension with flattery, our nobility with pride, our love of work with avarice, our good deeds with vanity, our worthiness with scorn of others, and our labors with ambition? Only those who have not accepted the spirit of this world, or have rejected it, who *do not love the world or the things in the world*, can accept the Spirit which is from God.

Can we be filled with the Holy Spirit if we are still so full of ourselves that there is not a single space within us for even a drop of the all-filling water, which in all directions springs *up into everlasting life*, to do anything but disappear or become clay through our self-love or our sinful remains? Our impurity is an obstruction that blocks the flow of the Spirit of the Lord, which is like the sources of spring waters sent to create a new world and *renew the face of the Earth*. But it is not because of wrath, but rather the mercy of God, that these sources do not flow into unworthy souls, for the holy and sanctifying water of life, having fallen on impurity, would consume it with an all-consuming fire. *John 4:14*

Psalm 103:30

Therefore, do not grumble against the Spirit of the Lord if you reject the flesh yourself and the world with all your strength and with a spiritual thirst come to Christ, but find that you cannot yet drink from the source of blessings, nor yet feel in yourselves the comforting presence of cooling and renewing grace, or else, having sensed it for a moment, have lost it. The Gospels tell us that while Jesus Christ Himself preached *concerning the Spirit, whom those believing in Him would receive; for the Holy Spirit was not yet given, because Jesus was not yet glorified*. In another place, He tells His disciples that even after they followed Him, they first had to be tested with the loss of His visible presence, and only then be able to rise up to mystical communion with the Holy Spirit: *It is to your advantage that I go away; for if I do not go away, the Helper will not come to you; but if I depart, I will send Him to you*. Even after His Resurrection, when *all authority [was] given to [Him] in Heaven and on Earth*, the Apostles needed fifty days of patience, of being in *one accord in prayer and supplication*, so that they might, having rejected all things, finally be filled with the Holy Spirit and begin to live in this fullness. Only having rejected everything were they found worthy to celebrate the great feast of God. *John 7:39*

John 16:7

Matthew 28:18
Acts 1:14

Perhaps in your case, though you desire the same apostolic inheritance in Christ, but do not feel in yourselves the same anointing in the Spirit, perhaps for you the Holy Spirit has not yet been given because Jesus has not yet been glorified in you. Perhaps you only accepted Him as a Prophet who bears the word of God in His mouth, but perhaps you have not yet consecrated yourselves to Him as to the High Priest, that in the communion of His universal sacrifice, He might raise you up to the blessed offering of His Father. Perhaps you have not yet praised Him as the King, in which case not a single desire or thought of yours would be allowed without His will. Perhaps it is to your advantage, for you still seek Christ *according to the flesh*, rather than the spirit, and for this reason the desired Bridegroom has been taken away from you for a time. This deprivation of spiritual consolation will purify your faith, will raise up your love, will strengthen your patience, will make your prayer subtle, will cast out the dangerous sense of self-satisfaction, and will prepare for you an even greater blessedness.

For those who do not yet sense the presence of the Spirit, at the very least *the anointing which you have received from Him abides in you, and you do not need that anyone teach you*. But what about us, who only live by flesh and blood, who *cannot inherit the Kingdom of God*? What shall we do, who are spiritually dead, cold, and dry, like those bones scattered about the field in Ezekiel's vision? *Can these bones live*? God asked the Prophet, desiring to send down on them His life-giving Spirit. *I have no pleasure in the death of the wicked, but that the wicked turn from his way and live*. Without a doubt, God looks down on our own spiritual bones and desires with the same mercy to bring us back to life by the Holy Spirit. '*Can these bones live?*' So, I answered, '*O Lord God, You know*'.

And so today, O Lord, speak these words Yourself, which the Prophet once spoke, speak to these bones: *Surely, I will cause breath to enter into you, and you shall live. I will put sinews on you and bring flesh upon you, cover you with skin and put breath in you; and you shall live. Then you shall know that I am the Lord*.

Amen!

Margin references:
- 2 Corinthians 5:16
- 2 Corinthians 5:16
- 1 John 2:27
- 1 Corinthians 15:50
- Ezekiel 37:3
- Ezekiel 33:11
- Ezekiel 37:3
- Ezekiel 37:5-6

26

Homily on the Descent of the Holy Spirit, after the blessing of the Church of the Annunciation of the Mother of God, which is better known for its side altar in honor of the Holy Unmercenaries Cosmas and Damian in Shubino (1842)

Continuing today to celebrate the memory of the descent of the Holy Spirit on the Apostles, and at the same time having been found worthy of triumphantly accomplishing the blessing of this temple, we have the fortunate opportunity to unite both events in our thoughts, and through this to enter a contemplation that for us will be both consoling and instructive.

The holy Evangelist Luke, when explaining the circumstances preceding the descent of the Holy Spirit on the Apostles, said that after the Lord's Ascension to Heaven, they returned from the Mount of Olives to Jerusalem, *and when they had entered, they went up into the upper room where they were staying. Later, these all continued with one accord in prayer and supplication, with the women and Mary the mother of Jesus, and with His brothers.* Finally, *When the day of Pentecost had fully come, they were all with one accord in one place.* What is this upper room in which the first Church of Christ waited? And what does the Apostles' waiting in this place actually mean? Was this a simple dwelling place in which people live day and night? That would not be possible, simply because of the large amount of people who are presented as being in this upper room. There were the Twelve Apostles, the most-pure Mother of God, the Myrrh-bearers and other pious women, and the other disciples of the Lord whom the evangelist counts as being *about a hundred and twenty.* Would it have been proper or even possible for all of them to live in a single upper room? And so, what was this upper room?

It reminds me of the one mentioned by the same Evangelist, *a large, furnished upper room,* in which the Lord told Peter and John to *make ready* for the Passover meal. In that upper room, He established, and for the first time performed, the mystery of His Body and Blood. Either this upper room is the same exact one, or it is the same kind of room, both in purpose and in dignity. Its purpose was not to be a place to live in and to sleep, to eat and spend an evening, or to sit and sleep; on the contrary, its purpose was to be a place where *all [could] continue with one accord in prayer and supplication.* This was a place for the performance of the Mystical Supper of the Lord; in it was also held the election of Matthias to the holy service of being one of the Twelve Apostles. This was the upper room which was higher than all that was earthly or quotidian; and those who remained there in pious spirit touched the heavenly and the divine, for which reason they finally received that greatest gift of all—triumphantly and miraculously, both Heaven and God Himself appeared in that room. The Holy Spirit not only inspired the Apostles with His all-powerful breath, and not only did He illumine them with tongues of fire, lighting their hearts with His fire and forming their tongues for the universal preaching of salvation, but even the very place of their abiding He filled with His holiness and grace: *it filled the whole house where they were sitting.* Acts 2:2

Once more I ask: what sort of upper room was this? I hope that what I have said already is enough to justify this final answer that I will give to the question: this upper room of Zion, the apostolic room, the place of the descent of the Holy Spirit is nothing other than the first image of the holy Christian temple; at the same time, it was a holy Christian temple. Consequently, today's newly-consecrated temple is a repetition, a renewal, a multiplication of the apostolic upper room of the descent of the Holy Spirit.

It is true, you may not have heard here the noise *as of a rushing mighty wind*; you may not have seen tongues of fire; and no one here speaks the various tongues of foreign nations. But consider that even in the apostolic upper room, that is, in the holy temple of the Apostles, not every day did they hear the frightening sound of a wind; it was only once that the fiery tongues appeared; however, in other times, this temple was not deprived of the grace of the Holy Spirit, which filled it daily. Acts 2:2

Without the initial miraculous wind and sparkle of fire, the holy Apostles continued to give the same gift of the Holy Spirit in their quiet laying on of hands that has continued, uninterrupted, until our own days. *Therefore tongues are for a sign, not to those who believe but to unbelievers.* In other words, the miraculous gift of speaking in unfamiliar foreign languages was sent by God for people who had not yet come to believe, so that through this sign of their spoken language, they would be given an instruction in faith and at the same time, through this miraculous gift, they would be confirmed in divine faith. 1 Corinthians 14:22

However, for those who have already come to believe, such a sign is unnecessary. The more the divine faith spread over all the Earth, the more the miraculous gift of tongues disappeared; consequently, the cessation of this gift is not a loss of grace, but a lack of need. The Lord does not approve of His believers seeking overt signs for confirmation of faith; on the contrary, He ascribes special worth to faith that doesn't require it. *Blessed are those who haven't seen and yet have believed.*

<small>John 20:29</small>

What shall we say, brethren? Do we dare to demand of God in our own temple that which was not always present in the apostolic temple, especially since it was not even always necessary? Why do we consider it a great loss for us if such miraculous signs do not appear here? Is not the word of Christ, which you hear in the Gospel, just as divine as the tongues of fire coming from the Holy Spirit? Is it not the same Body and Blood of Christ on the table of this altar as it was in the upper room of Zion? In prayers and service, which are here performed according to the tradition of the Apostles, is not the same Holy Spirit present, illumining, sanctifying, transforming the earthly into the heavenly, the material into the spiritual, the created into the divine?

Is it not by His coming that the waters of baptism are blessed, that the oil of unction is sanctified? Was it not He who entered and came to dwell in this temple through the relics of His Saints, whose bodies, according to His own testimony, are *the temple of the Holy Spirit who is in you*? Do we need anything more for our faith, reverence, love, consolation, and hope? Let us believe in the grace of this temple without daring to ask for a vision of miracles. Let us be reverent, for truly *the Lord is in His holy temple.* Let us come to love *the beauty of [the Lord's] house*, not merely the material and visible temple, but the immaterial and spiritual one. Let us be glad, together with David, who said, *Let us go into the house of the Lord.* Let us have hope that the Lord, and, as He did for many before us, the Lord will shelter us *in the secret place of His dwelling...in the day of [our] trouble,* in the evil day of sin, covering us from the horrors of justice by the mystery of the grace of forgiveness. In the evil day of the temporary punishment, may He cover us who run to the mystery of His inner dwelling place

<small>1 Corinthians 6:19</small>

<small>Psalm 10:3</small>
<small>Psalm 25:8</small>

<small>Psalm 121:1</small>

<small>Psalm 27:5</small>

through the sincere prayer of the heart, may he preserve us in the grace of protection, consolation, redemption.

It is consoling to find, to recognize, and to examine the mystical similarity between the grace-filled temple of Christians and the miraculous apostolic upper room of the descent of the Holy Spirit. But to make this consolation full and complete, it is necessary to make another comparison — between those who prayed in that upper room and those who stand in our temple here today.

All that the apostolic upper room had that is exalted and desirable was a gift of God, a gift that the Apostles themselves did not desire, since who can properly do anything to make God his debtor, when God has no need of anything from us? After all, He is the God whom all creation serves not through its own property, but through His gifts. These gifts are not denied us either, for *The Lord is merciful and gracious, long-suffering, and of great kindness.* *Psalm 144:9*

However, these gifts would not have been given if there were no hands extended toward Him in expectation. The treasure would not have been given if there were no vessels, as clean and prepared as possible, ready for it, which the Apostles and the others who waited with them were. Insofar as we become similar to the Apostles and their fellow recipients of grace in terms of our disposition of soul and heart, we approach the divine treasure of grace.

What is this disposition of soul and heart? *They were all with one accord in one place. These all continued with one accord in prayer and supplication.* The Apostles and the disciples of the Lord remained in prayer and supplication to God, thereby preparing themselves to accept the grace of the Holy Spirit. Let us also remember that the Lord, before His Ascension, did not give them any special command concerning prayer, but simply commanded them *not to depart from Jerusalem, but to wait for the promise of the Father*, that is, the promised Holy Spirit. What was the purpose, you might ask, of praying for something that is already promised *Acts 2:1* *Acts 1:14* *Acts 1:4* and which cannot fail to be fulfilled by a God who is faithful in His promises? And yet, the Apostles and disciples of the Lord prayed for the Promised One because they felt an internal necessity to do so, even if it seems like they were asking for something not yet promised, only hoped for. This internal compulsion is necessary for the acquisition of grace. Prayer is the breath of the spiritual man.

Just as the earthly man attracts the surrounding air into himself by breathing in, so the soul opens itself by prayer to the omnipresent Spirit of God, accepting from Him life and spiritual power. Let us then abide in prayer and supplication, so that our heavenly Father, according to the promise of His Only-begotten Son, *will...give the Holy Spirit to those who ask Him*. The Apostles and disciples of the Lord were persistent in prayer, that is, they continued in it constantly, without stopping or growing tired. It was not a single all-night vigil that they served after the Ascension of Christ; day after day they served, while the promise was not yet fulfilled. But they did not complain about the wait; they did not doubt the promise, though it was unfulfilled for days. They did not become exhausted; they did not become lazy; they continued to pray just as fervently on the tenth day as on the first.

Luke 11:13

Finally, their patience was justified, and their prayer was triumphantly answered. And so, let us also not be impatient in our prayers, neither let us not be lazy or faithless. Let us run to prayer as often as possible; let us remain in it as constantly as possible; let us not lose faith when we do not see quickly ripening fruits from our prayer. Whether slowly or quickly, whether openly or mystically, the Lord will give us, who persist in prayer, the necessary grace for our salvation.

The Apostles and disciples of the Lord remained "with one accord in one place." Such a gathering was commanded by Christ Himself, when He said, *If two of you agree on Earth concerning anything that they ask, it will be done for them by My Father in Heaven. For where two or three are gathered together in My name, I am there in the midst of them*. An important aspect of prayer is the single-mind-

Matthew 18:19-20

edness of those who pray. Similar to the power of the Holy Spirit in His miraculous descent, the power of the combined prayer of the apostolic Church was effective many times both in spiritual and natural realities. By it, *the place where they were assembled together was shaken.* At another time, this prayer loosened bonds and chains, opening the doors of the prison holding the Apostle Peter. Why else do we pray together in Church in our own time, except to increase the power of each individual prayer through the intercession of many who pray together *with one accord in one place?*

Acts 4:31

Acts 2:1

Let us not be ashamed or be afraid to admit that my prayer or your prayer is weak and unworthy to receive the grace we ask for. But come, place your two cents of prayer into the treasure-house of single-souled communal prayer, and this combined treasure will be enough to buy for all of us the precious gem of the grace of God. Thanks to God, even today, we do not lack examples of how the insistent prayer of the Church, the sincere prayer of Christians gathered together in one mind and heart, can "bring a soul out of the prison" of temptations, delusions, passions, and sins, *that [we] may give thanks to the Name of the Lord.*

Paraphrase of Psalm 141:8

And for this reason, with hope and boldness, let us beseech You today with the combined voice of believing souls, "O Heavenly King, Spirit of truth, come and abide in us!" Do not cease to overshadow this temple with Your grace, for You have blessed it on this day, the day of Your descent. Fulfill for good all the desires of those who enter it with faith and prayer. Illumine their minds with the light of truth, warm their hearts with love for all that is good, especially for You Yourself, the Source of all good things! Do good to those souls who have come to love the beauty of this Your house; and to all who have sacrificed the earthly for the sake of the heavenly, give Your earthly and heavenly blessing. Save all of our souls, so that in unending joy we may glorify You together with the Father who is without beginning and His Only-begotten Son, unto the ages of ages. Amen.

www.ingramcontent.com/pod-product-compliance
Lightning Source LLC
Chambersburg PA
CBHW020532080526
44583CB00013B/828